Varvara Tzika

Ranking classifieds at Marktplaats

AF138571

Varvara Tzika

Ranking classifieds at Marktplaats

Query Modeling, Retrieval Methods, Data Fusion and Result Diversification

LAP LAMBERT Academic Publishing

Impressum / Imprint
Bibliografische Information der Deutschen Nationalbibliothek: Die Deutsche Nationalbibliothek verzeichnet diese Publikation in der Deutschen Nationalbibliografie; detaillierte bibliografische Daten sind im Internet über http://dnb.d-nb.de abrufbar.
Alle in diesem Buch genannten Marken und Produktnamen unterliegen warenzeichen-, marken- oder patentrechtlichem Schutz bzw. sind Warenzeichen oder eingetragene Warenzeichen der jeweiligen Inhaber. Die Wiedergabe von Marken, Produktnamen, Gebrauchsnamen, Handelsnamen, Warenbezeichnungen u.s.w. in diesem Werk berechtigt auch ohne besondere Kennzeichnung nicht zu der Annahme, dass solche Namen im Sinne der Warenzeichen- und Markenschutzgesetzgebung als frei zu betrachten wären und daher von jedermann benutzt werden dürften.

Bibliographic information published by the Deutsche Nationalbibliothek: The Deutsche Nationalbibliothek lists this publication in the Deutsche Nationalbibliografie; detailed bibliographic data are available in the Internet at http://dnb.d-nb.de.
Any brand names and product names mentioned in this book are subject to trademark, brand or patent protection and are trademarks or registered trademarks of their respective holders. The use of brand names, product names, common names, trade names, product descriptions etc. even without a particular marking in this work is in no way to be construed to mean that such names may be regarded as unrestricted in respect of trademark and brand protection legislation and could thus be used by anyone.

Coverbild / Cover image: www.ingimage.com

Verlag / Publisher:
LAP LAMBERT Academic Publishing
ist ein Imprint der / is a trademark of
OmniScriptum GmbH & Co. KG
Heinrich-Böcking-Str. 6-8, 66121 Saarbrücken, Deutschland / Germany
Email: info@lap-publishing.com

Herstellung: siehe letzte Seite /
Printed at: see last page
ISBN: 978-3-659-68246-9

Zugl. / Approved by: University of Amsterdam, Master of Science thesis

Copyright © 2015 OmniScriptum GmbH & Co. KG
Alle Rechte vorbehalten. / All rights reserved. Saarbrücken 2015

Dedicated to my lovely family, my nephews and my partner
Alexis for their unconditional support.

Acknowledgements

I would like to express my gratitude to Manos Tsagkias, Ton Wessling and Vadim Zaytsev. The work included in this book would not have been possible if not for their assistance, patience and support.

Contents

Chapter 1

Introduction

Marktplaats is an e-commerce platform where users are able to sell products or services by creating classifieds. Classifieds are a way for users to list their items, services, or properties for sale without creating an auction-style or fixed price listing. One of Marktplaats main goals is to keep their users satisfied so they can improve their reputation and revenues. To keep users satisfied, they want to help them find the most relevant product or service as quickly as possible. Users are searching for available classifieds with a word or sentence that represent the query. However, these words can be interpreted in multiple ways and using these words in a query results in ambiguity. Ambiguous queries with a short query length in a large amount of classifieds produces a big and broad list of proposed classifieds. For instance the word Java can be interpreted as Java island or Java programming language or Java coffee and all of their related classifieds will be retrieved by the search engine [44]. If users are provided with a broad list of classifieds, they will spend a lot of time to find what they need. Instead, providing them with a small and concrete list with classifieds will save them time. Taking into account that users are examining a classified (reading its contents) only when it appeals to them, we are attempting to solve that problem by retrieving and recommending to users a list of relevant classifieds based on the previously examined classified. A classified consists of content describing elements (fields) such as title, description, category and attributes that are created by the sellers. The previously visited classified fields contain additional information that help us retrieve a list with classifieds.

Many companies had to come up with related solutions to problems like this. Google News groups news by story rather than presenting a raw listing of all articles. Also, they record every click or search that every user made and just below the "Top Stories" section users can see a section labeled "Recommended for your email address" along with three stories that are recommended to them based on their past click history. This way Google uses users history to predict their interest and give better recommendations [39]. Likewise, Amazon based on users past shopping history and site activity recommends books and other items likely to be of interest. Also, Amazon is mapping items to the list of similar items. For example, if there is a list with 3 items that a user is interested in, then this becomes an item list. If another user is interested in one of these items, then the rest of the items in the list will be recommended to him as well [45]. In the music industry, Schlitter and Falkowski use data from Last.fm and create user profiles based on the genres of the most listened artists [40]. They create communities based on the categorization and they recommend music to users based on the category of the community they belong to. For example, one community is hip hop and its members are recommended to listen to hip hop music [41].

Previously described companies solve the problem in different ways which we could use as well. One of the options is to classify items in categories as done by Last.fm. However, trawling through hundreds or thousands of categories and subcategories of data is not an efficient method for finding information [42]. Another option is to use a recommendation algorithm based on other users history but then we have to deal also with new users that don't have any history to relate with others. Another constraint is that classifieds are not active for a long time, thus making recommendations based on user history is difficult. Offline solutions such as Amazon's which generates similar item lists periodically, is not useful with classifieds because of their short life span. We could also use the click logs to improve the ranking of the search results via the use of the so called learning to rank methods, however these methods rely on already optimal search algorithms that are currently lacking at Marktplaats. Our goal is first to explore the utility of several retrieval methods for retrieving relevant classifieds. In future work we will explore click models and learning to rank approaches.

To show to user relevant classifieds based on their interest requires finding the relevant classifieds based on their history and to relate the information we have with other classifieds. Recommending similar classifieds to users, involves retrieving the most important information of the classified which the users have already seen. Classifieds have this information either on their description or in their attributes. Extracting this knowledge from enormous amounts of data can be achieved with methods from the information retrieval area which is defined as "the area of study concerned with searching for documents, for information within documents, and for metadata about documents" [43].

To implement this approach we extract terms of a classified that represent the information need of the user. This procedure is called query modeling. Then, given a retrieval strategy and a query, the search engine responds with a list with classifieds. The retrieval strategy is responsible to search in our indexed classifieds based on the input (query) and they will produce the list

6

with similar classifieds (result list).

A good choice of the retrieval strategy or the query modeling will be proved once adequate lists are constructed based on the input that we gave. Different query models will result in a different result list. Different retrieval strategies will result in different result lists as well. The choice of the best query model and retrieval strategy are subjects of experimentation. The results the models give us will affect the performance and the accuracy of the system. A good performing system will be evaluated based on the precision of the system. That means that it will be affected by the number of relevant results retrieved by a system and the ordering (rank). System is the combination of the query modeling, retrieval strategy and all the systemic properties like how did we process the classified (e.g. removing noise words like 'the', 'or' etc.). Our work is implemented on a company, where data and different kind of users can help us to evaluate different query models.

Different query models will be created based on different combination of the visited classifieds fields. Also, we can extract discriminative terms of the visited classified to represent the information need. Furthermore, we can take feedback from a result list and create a new query that will result a new list which is the recommendation.

Retrieval strategies have existed since the early 90's and there is no need to create a new one. In this work we will examine three popular retrieval strategies, TfIdf, Okapi BM25F and LM. We will investigate which strategy will increase the performance of our systems.

In a large amount of classifieds it is possible that there are lots of possible redundant or containing partially or fully duplicative information. Our goal is to expose less classifieds with high potential to cover the information need of the user. Experiments will be conducted to find the best way to provide a diversified result lists instead of a list with lots of duplicated classifieds. Since user's information need are often ambiguous, we can give to the user more diversified results to increase the possibility that a classified will satisfy their information need.

Merging the result lists that are retrieved by multiple query models to one new list improves the performance of individual systems [32]. Experiments with multiple late fusion techniques are provided. We also use fusion methods on the diversified result lists to compare and see if there is any improvement.

To conclude, we derive multiple query models from a given classified, which are then used to retrieve similar classifieds from an index, resulting in multiple ranked lists. We then diversify these lists. Then we merge this initial lists as well as the diversified lists using data fusion techniques. Query models are created by exploiting the structure of the given classified and by discriminative terms of the classifieds context.

The research questions we aim to answer are the following:

1. Which query model improves the performance of title query model?

2. Which of the three (TfIdf, Okapi BM25F, LM) ranking algorithms is performing better?

3. Does the fusion of individual strategies improve the performance of the individuals query models?

4. Are the results of diversification affected if only the similarity with the previous displayed classified is taken into account?

5. Are the results of diversification affected if the average similarity of previous displayed docs is taken into account?

6. Are the results of diversification affected if only the similarity with the previous four displayed classifieds is taken into account?

7. Does the fusion of previously diversified ranked lists outperforms the system performance of fusing the non-diversified systems?

The remainder of this work is organized as follows. In the second section we describe related work. In the third section we revisit core concepts of information retrieval and explain important aspects of the method that we follow. Section four presents the experimental framework. The fifth section offers experimental results. Section six analyzes the results and the seventh section concludes this work and discusses future directions.

Chapter 2

Background

We distinguish between the following areas of research of related work: query modeling, data fusion, diversification, data fusion of diversified result lists. Additionally, we are presenting our contribution on these areas.

2.1 Related work on query modeling

Related work on query representations exists from the early 90's. From the first Text REtrieval Conferences (TREC) query representation using terms of the topic and routing queries are used [22], [23]. Deepening on the TREC conferences, in 1993, one of the TREC2 experiments was the combination of multiple representations and different treatment of key concepts of a topic like title, description etc. but the effect of adding the description in the title query model is not documented. However, it is proven that automatic creation of a query representation is as effective as a manually chosen one [23].

Multiple types of information source have been considered as input to the query creation. Similar to our approach, Balog et all on [46] are doing query expansion by using sample documents. Other source of information source that are used are tags, categories, history logs etc [47].

More work exists in [24] that different query representations are experimented like routing queries, Ad hoc and phrases queries and proved that combining multiple queries are useful. In 1957, Luhn [25] suggested that automatic text retrieval systems could be designed based on a comparison of content identifiers attached both to the stored texts and to the users information queries.

2.2 Related work on diversification

Related work in diversification of results started when it was understood that the ranking of the search engines was not enough to cover the information need of different users. Multiple ways of diversifying results were proposed. In 1998 Carbonell and Gordstein [26] introduced the Maximal Marginal Relevance (MMR) which takes into account the relevance of the document but also the similarity between the other documents. Agrawal et al. in [27], focused on how to diversify search results given ambiguous queries based on the category the results belong. Zhai and Laferty in [28] proposed to include some results for each subtopic of the search results to achieve diversification. In [29] they proposed to rank the results with a goal to maximize the probability of finding a relevant document among the top N so they can achieve perfect precision using probabilistic model from the Bayesian information retrieval techniques.

Furthermore, an implementation on diversification exists in [30]. They demonstrate a tool which uses different kinds of diversification. The tool gives the opportunity to the user to select how to combine relevance with diversity. The choices for diversification of the results are based on context, novelty or different categories. The user can see how the results are affected by using diversification.

2.3   Related work on data fusion

On the early years of TREC conferences the effectiveness of the result sets fusion was investigated as well. Belkin in [32], conducted experiments with combSUM, combMNZ, combANZ, combMIN, combMAX data fusion techniques in two ways. The first was for the combination of query formulations and the second for the combination of two different data collections. They concluded that combining multiple pieces of evidence as query formulations is a beneficial way to increase retrieval effectiveness.

Lee in [33] influenced by Belkin investigated the evidence that different runs retrieve similar sets of relevant documents and different sets of non-relevant documents and how this evidence affects the system performance. Also, he evaluated existing data fusion techniques (combSUM, combMNZ, combANZ, combMIN, combMAX) and combGMNZ using different similarity algorithms as well as query formulations. It is proved that CombMNZ provides better retrieval effectiveness than the others because combMNZ favors documents retrieved by multiple runs. He also identified that in the case of combination of multiple runs, higher relevance overlap than non-relevance overlap on the retrieved set can improve system effectiveness. Lee did not identify the exact difference needed to improve effectiveness. Also, he did not use the most effective result sets available, but rather, selected his test sets at random. Furthermore, he used result sets from entirely different information retrieval systems. This does not simply vary the retrieval strategy used for the experiments, but all retrieval utilities and other systemic differences.

Chowdhury in [34] investigated the fusion of highly effective retrieval strategies keeping the systemic properties stable. He concluded that it doesn't tend to improve retrieval effectiveness but he used a limited amount of data and query models.

Beitzel et al [35] experimented with high effective retrieval strategies as well as to clarify the conditions required to improve effectiveness of data fusion. He concluded that significant number of unique relevant docs is required, not a simple difference between relevant and non-relevant overlap as previously thought. From these results, it is clear that voting is highly detrimental to fusion in the case of fusing highly effective retrieval strategies in the same system. On the other hand, in [36] they proved the opposite. They keep stable the systemic properties like query modeling, stemming, document presentation etc and they experiment with different highly effective retrieval strategies. Their goal was to prove that the believe that the combination of highly effective retrieval systems is an effective way to fuse result sets. They have shown effectiveness cannot be improved by fusing highly effective retrieval strategies.

Other related work on data fusion can be found on [37] they explained and contacted experiments with three data fusion algorithms (Rank position, Boda count, and Condorcet). The first one takes into account the position of the results and the other two are voting the results. They also contact experiments using the best, bias and all systems.

The first attempt to utilize data fusion for diversification was in [38]. They proposed their fusion method and they prove that data fusion outperforms the existing diversification methods. However, there is no related work on fusion of diversified results.

2.4   Our contribution

Our contribution to the query modeling topic is that we compare multiple retrieval systems taking into account different systemic properties like query models, retrieval strategies and preprocessing.

On fusion of the results, we used combMNZ to fuse results with stable systemic differences but with different retrieval algorithms. The approach is the same as Chowdhury in [34]. We will investigate whether his conclusion that fusion of retrieval strategies doesn't improve retrieval effectiveness also applies when using description, attributes and category fields from classifieds on the query models instead of only the title.

On diversification of results, we will investigate the impact on performance of comparing a specific document set instead of comparing the similarity of the entire set of documents. Also, proposing three alternative diversification methods, we will investigate the impact on diversification of using window on comparing classifieds.

In a similar approach to Liang et al where they proposed to diversify fused result lists, we merge diversified results [38]. To the best of our knowledge, the fusion of diversified results is not investigated yet. So this is the first attempt to see if the performance of diversified results is affected by the data fusion.

Having presented the related work of each part of our approach and our contribution, we can now continue explaining what is our methodology in the next chapter.

Chapter 3

Methods

In this section, we describe the methods used in the approach we follow.

3.1 Query modeling

A query is the representation of a user's information need. Enhancing the query by changing or expanding it is called query modeling. Query modeling creation involves the preprocessing step and the identification of tokens. The right query model is the most important element that will affect the resulting classified list. There are several ways of query modeling. We explore three different kinds: a) exploiting the previously visited classified structure b) extracting discriminative terms based on the log likelihood ratio and c) expanding queries by using pseudo relevance feedback.

3.1.1 Exploiting the classified structure

The previously visited classified is an indication of the user's interest. Thus, important information can be extracted from this visited or source classified for creating query models. Classifieds typically consist of title, description and category. Some classifieds also consist of attributes specific to the category. We believe that each field has different information and using this information can enhance our results. The title summarizes the contents of the classified. It only consists of a few important words and we assume that using these words in the query model will retrieve highly relevant classifieds. Description is a more detailed representation of the classified. We assume that using words from the description in the query model will retrieve a broader result than using the title's words. Also, description contains more noise than the title's contents due to the amount of words it contains and we believe that we will retrieve a lot of irrelevant documents in the query model by using only description. From the other side, combining title words with description words will give a boost in the words that are present in both fields and it will expand the result list with classifieds matching the description words that don't exist in the title. Category is the category that classified is part of and is very generic. Using category words in our query model will retrieve a broad list of classifieds that don't cover our scope to find the most relevant classifieds first. We assume though that combining the attributes with categories can retrieve relevant classifieds. Furthermore, we believe that combining all these fields together will result the most relevant classifieds list. Category and attributes fields consist of different information than description and title and combining them means that we have a full descriptive representation of our visited classified which increases the chances to retrieve a highly relevant classifieds list. The combination of content fields that are mapped to queries and multiple query models are presented in table 3.1.

Table 3.1: A summary of the query models we consider is presented. We mark the classifieds fields we use on the term extraction and weather we use log likelihood ratio (LLR), pseudo relevance feedback (PRF), stemming or not.

Name	Fields	Stemming	LLR	PRF
T	title	no	no	no
T-LLR	title	no	yes	no
T stemming	title	yes	no	no
T-LLR stemming	title	yes	yes	no
T+D	title, description	no	no	no
T+D+A+C	title, description, category, attributes	no	no	no
A+C	attributes, category	no	no	no
T+D+A+C-LLR	title, description, category, attributes	no	yes	no
T+D+A+C-Pseudo	title, description, category, attributes	no	no	yes
T-Pseudo	title	no	no	yes

3.1.2   Pseudo relevance feedback

The general idea behind relevance feedback is to take feedback from the top results that are initially retrieved from a given query. Although, pseudo relevance feedback improves the efficiency of the system, it is dependable to the initial query since it assumes that the top k results are relevant. However, through query expansion, some relevant documents that are missed in the initial round can then be retrieved to improve the overall performance. Clearly, the effect of this method strongly relies on the quality of the selected expansion terms but we assume that our initially retrieved classifieds list will be improved.

3.1.3 Log likelihood ratio

Term extraction is a key component in query modeling i.e. which are the right terms for retrieving classifieds that address the user's information need? A few methods exist to retrieve discriminative terms like idf or Log likelihood ratio. We consider the log likelihood ratio (LLR) and we create query models by using terms extracted with this method from the visited classified.

"A likelihood ratio test is a statistical test used to compare the fit of two models, one of which (the null model) is a special case of the other (the alternative model). The test is based on the likelihood ratio, which expresses how many times more likely the data are under one model than the other."

As it is described in [9] we can use LLR to compare corpora and find the terms of a corpus that are more characteristic. There are two main types of corpus comparison:

. Comparison of a sample corpus to a larger corpus (normative)

. Comparison of two (roughly) equal sized corpora

These two main types of comparison can be extended to the comparison of more than two corpora. For example, we may compare one normative corpus to several smaller corpora at the same time, or compare three or more equal sized corpora to each other. In general, however, this makes the results more difficult to interpret.

This first type of comparison is intended to discover features in the sample corpus with significantly different usage (i.e. frequency) to that found in "general" language. While second type aims to discover features in the corpora that distinguish one from another. In our case, the first type is more appropriate since we need to find a way to distinguish a model for a classified against a large corpus that will give us enough feedback for every word in the classified. We refer to the larger corpus as a "normative" corpus since it provides a text norm (or standard) against which we can compare.

The representativeness of the big corpus needs to be considered when comparing two corpora. It should contain samples of all major text types and if possible in some way proportional to their usage in the natural writing of a classified in case we want features (in our case frequencies) to make sense . In the case of classifieds created by users, we need a corpora with a data set of classifieds really created by users and big to contain almost all different words a user will write in his classified [9].

We can create query models with the use of LLR using the top k words with the biggest LLR number. This means that we have to calculate LL for every word in a given classified.

The method that we have to follow is the following: Given a visited classified as null corpora and a big dataset of classifieds as normative corpora that we wish to compare with, we produce a frequency list. This would be a word frequency list. For each word in the first frequency list we calculate the log-likelihood statistic. This is performed by constructing a contingency table see table 3.2.

Table 3.2: Contingency table for Log likelihood calculation.

	First Corpus	Second Corpus	Total
Frequency of word	a	b	a+b
Frequency of other words	c-a	d-b	c+d-a-b
Total	c	d	c+d

Then, we need to calculate the expected values (E) according to the following formula:

$$E_i = \frac{N_i \sum_i O_i}{\sum_i N_i} \qquad (3.1)$$

The calculation for the expected values takes into account the size of the two corpora, so we do not need to normalize the figures before applying the formula. We can then calculate the log-likelihood value according to this formula:

$$-2ln\lambda = 2\sum_i O_i ln\frac{O_i}{E_i} \qquad (3.2)$$

This equates to calculating log-likelihood LL as follows:

$$LL = 2 * ((a * ln\frac{a}{E1}) + (b * ln\frac{b}{E2})) \qquad (3.3)$$

The word frequency list is then sorted by the resulting LL values. This gives the effect of placing the largest LL value at the top of the list representing the word which has the most significant relative frequency difference between the two corpora. In this way, we can find the words most indicative (or characteristic) of one corpus, as compared to the other corpus, at the top of the list [9].

3.2 Retrieval models

A retrieval model takes a query and a classified as input and identifies a measure of relevance between the query and the classified. Different retrieval models have different retrieval strategies thus resulted documents differs as well.

Retrieval model or ranking function used by search engines mostly. A search engine except of finding the relevant document, has to rank and order them by relevance. This is typically done by assigning a numerical score to each document based on a ranking function, which incorporates features of the document, the query, and the overall document collection.

The study of retrieval models is central to information retrieval. Many different retrieval models have been proposed and tested, including vector space models, probabilistic models and logic-based model.

The ranking functions-retrieval models that we will use for this project are the following:

. TfIdf

. Okapi BM25

. Probabilistic Language Model

3.2.1   TfIdf

TfIdf (term frequency-inverse document frequency) used as term weighting factor in information retrieval. This retrieval method ranks documents based on characteristic terms of a document. Characteristic terms for a document are those who only frequently appear in the possible relevant document while infrequently in the rest documents of data collection [4].

TF is the frequency and idf is its inverse document frequency. Term frequency in a given document is the number of times a given term appears in that document. The inverse document frequency is a measure of whether the term is common or rare across all documents.

TfIdf is calculated as:

$$TfIdf = tf * idf \qquad (3.4)$$

$$idf = log\frac{d}{d_t} \qquad (3.5)$$

Where d is the total number of documents in the collection, d_t is the total number of documents where term t occurs. However if the term t does not occur in the document collection idf, then dt will be equal to zero. Therefore the formula is adjusted to 1+dt. The advantage of TfIdf is that it tends to filter out common terms. When a document has high term frequency while the term appears rarely in the whole collection of documents then it has high weight in TfIdf scoring.

3.2.2 Okapi BM25

In information retrieval, Okapi Best match 25 (BM25) is a ranking function used by search engines to rank matching documents according to their relevance to a given search query. Okapi ranking function is based on the probabilistic retrieval framework. It makes an estimation of the probability of finding if a document dj is relevant to a query q. Three factors affects Okapi's score. First is the query terms frequency, second is the inverted frequency of query terms and finally, the length of the document. With this way, it scores higher a short document that mention all query terms.

Given a query , containing keywords , the BM25 score of a document is:

$$BM25(d_j, q_i : N) = \frac{Idf(q_i) * Tf(q_i, d_j) * (k + 1)}{(tf(q_i, dj) + k * (1 - b + (b * |d_j|/L)))} \qquad (3.6)$$

Where N is the total number of documents, tf(q_i, d_j) is the frequency of q_i word in d_j document and idf(q_i) is the inverse document frequency of word given by:

$$idf(q_i) = log\frac{N - DF(q_i) + 0.5}{DF(q_i) + 0.5} \qquad (3.7)$$

Where d_j is the length of document d_j in words, L is the average document length in the corpus.

3.2.3 Language modeling

Language Modeling estimates the probability distribution of linguistic units such as words, sentences, queries, utterances, or even complete documents. The probability distribution itself is referred to as a language model [6]. Given the query q and the user U, we want to find the most probable documents. That is, we want to rank the documents by p($d|q$, U). Using Bayes' theorem:

$$p(d|q, U) = \frac{p(d|U)p(q|d, U)}{p(q|U)} \qquad (3.8)$$

For the purposes of ranking, we can ignore the denominator and define the relevance of a document as:

$$pq(d) = p(d|U) * p(q|d, U) \qquad (3.9)$$

The query likelihood p($q|d$) is calculated by assuming that the query terms are independent, and then multiplying the probabilities for the individual terms. If the query q = ($q_1 q_2 \ldots q_m$) , then:

$$p(q|d) = \prod_{i->1}^{m} q_i$$

Furthermore, suppose that we have the query "This is a great book for retrieval and evaluation in IR" created by the description of a book and also we have as candidate document with description "This is a book for evaluation in IR". The candidate document does not contain the query word "retrieval". Now, if we estimate $p(retrieval|d)$,then this probability will be zero and the query likelihood will vanish. Thus, the language model for a document has to distribute some probability mass among words that are not in the document too. This task is called smoothing [7]. Dirichlet smoothing is used to solve the zero probability and data sparseness problems.

$$p(q|d) = \frac{tf + m * p(q|C)}{|D| + m} \qquad (3.10)$$

3.3   Diversification

Maximal marginal relevance

Diversification is implemented to provide of more diversified result set. Maximal Marginal Relevance (MMR) is a diversification method aims to re-rank the result set selecting the highest combination of a similarity score between classifieds and their initial rank. It is defined as:

$$MMR \overset{def}{=} \underset{D_i \in R \setminus S}{\text{Arg max}}[\lambda(Sim_1(Di, Q) - (1 - \lambda)\underset{D_j \in S}{\max}Sim_2(D_i, D_j)] \qquad (3.11)$$

where: R : Rank list of documents retrieved by an IR system
S : is the subset of documents in R already selected
Sim1 : is the similarity between documents and a query
Sim2 : the similarity between the documents
λ : 0.5 because we want to give the same weight to ranking order and diversity

3.3.1   Maximal marginal relevance alternative 1

We introduce a flavor of MMR called Maximal Marginal Relevance alternative (MMRalt). It is a diversification method aims to re-rank the result set selecting the highest combination of a similarity score between pairs of classifieds and their initial rank. The main difference with MMR is that MMRalt will result a list with consecutive diversified pairs of classifieds.

$$MMRAlt \stackrel{def}{=} \operatorname*{Arg\ max}_{D_i \in R \setminus S}[\lambda(Sim_1(Di, Q) - (1 - \lambda)Sim_2(D_i, D_s)] \quad (3.12)$$

R : Rank list of documents retrieved by an IR system
S : is the subset of documents in R already selected
s : is the previous document selected
Sim1 : is the similarity between documents and a query
Sim2 : the similarity between the documents
λ : 0.5 because we want to give the same weight to ranking order and diversity

Data: Given the initially ranked classifieds list
Result: A diversified ranked classifieds list
initialization;
while *we still have non selected classifieds in the given list* **do**
  choose the first one and expose it
  $alreadydisplayedlist \leftarrow classifiedinthefirstrankedposition$
  calculate the MMR of documentX using as cosine similarity the similarity between X and already displayed expose the classifiedZ with the max(MMR) as the next one $alreadydisplayed \leftarrow classifiedZ$
  remove the classifiedZ of the given list
end

Algorithm 1: MMRalt algorithm.

3.3.2 Maximal marginal relevance alternative 2

We introduce an alternative flavor of the MMR algorithm, the Maximal Marginal Relevance alternative 2 (MMRalt2). This diversification method aims to rerank the result set selecting the highest combination of a similarity score between classifieds and their initial rank. The difference between MMR and MMRalt2 is that this technique does not take into account the maximum cosine similarity between a classifies and the displayed classifieds. Instead it takes into account the average MMRalt2 score between a document and the previously displayed classifieds. The difference between MMRalt and MMRalt2 is that the later aims to have the entire result list diversified. The hypothesis here is that taking into account the average MMR score between all the previously ranked classifieds and the next proposed classified is a better indication of similarity than the MAX cosine similarity.

$$MMRAlt2 \stackrel{def}{=} \underset{D_i \in R, s}{\text{Arg max}} \qquad (3.13)$$

R :Rank list of documents retrieved by an IR system

S :is the previous document selected

Data: Given the initially ranked classifieds list
Result: A diversified ranked classifieds list
initialization;
while *we still have non selected classifieds in the given list* **do**

> choose the first one and expose it
> $doc_selected \leftarrow classifiedinthefirstrankedposition$
> $MMRx \leftarrow AVG(MMR_doc_selected)$ expose the classifiedZ with the
> max(MMR) as the next one $alreadydisplayed \leftarrow classifiedZ$ remove
> the classifiedZ of the given list

end

Algorithm 2: MMRalt2 algorithm.

3.3.3 Maximal marginal relevance within a range of four classifieds

This proposed algorithm which we called MMRalt2last4 is a diversification method which aims to re-rank the result set by selecting the highest combination of a similarity score between the last four re-ranked classifieds and their initial rank. The main difference between the other approaches is that this technique takes into account only the last four selected documents instead of all of them. The resulted list with similar classifieds that Marktplaats decided to expose will be in pages consisting of four classifieds. With our proposed way, each page will always consist of diversified results and the initial rank will not be affected as much as the other approaches.

Data: Given the initially ranked classifieds list
Result: A diversified ranked classifieds list
initialization;
$doc_selected \leftarrow classifiedinthefirstrankedposition$
while *we still have non selected classifieds in the given list* **do**
| choose the first one and expose it
| $doc_selected \leftarrow classifiedinthefirstrankedposition$
| $MMRx \leftarrow AVG(MMR_{d}oc_selected_{last four})$ expose the classifiedZ
| with the max(MMR) as the next one $alreadydisplayed \leftarrow classifiedZ$
| remove the classifiedZ of the given list
end

Algorithm 3: MMRalt2last4 algorithm.

3.4 Late data fusion

Based on [10], data fusion is the process of integration of multiple data and knowledge representing the same real-world object into a consistent, accurate, and useful representation. There are two approaches for the combination of data known as early fusion or late fusion. Early fusion is the combination of data prior to indexing. Thus the data aggregated and then retrieval model use this aggregated data as input. While late fusion assumes each source of data has associated with it some form of a ranking function, each of which can be independently queried. Once each source has been queried, the outputs of each of these queries can be aggregated together to form a final response to the initial query.

Since different retrieval results can generate quite different ranges of similarity values, a normalization method should be applied to each retrieval result. Normalization controls the ranges of similarity values that retrieval systems generate. Hence, in order to align both the lower bounds of similarity values and the upper, we normalize each similarity value by the maximum and minimum actually seen in a retrieval result as follows:

$$normalizedscore(x) = \frac{x - min}{max - min} \qquad (3.14)$$

Where min is the minimum value for the ranked list and max is the maximum value for the ranked list. After the normalization of the score we merged all of the ranked lists. We consider the following late data fusion methods explained on table 3.3:

Table 3.3: Late data fusion methods we consider.

Name	Explanation
combMAX	Maximum of individual scores
combMIN	Minimum of individual scores
combSUM	Sum of individual scores
combANZ	combSUM / number of non zero scores
combMNZ	combSUM * number of non zero scores
WcombSUM	weighted sum of individual scores
WcombMNZ	WcombSUM * count of non zero results
WcombWW	WcombSUM * sum of individual weights

Then, we diversify all of the merged ranked lists using the diversification methods described above.

Next chapter will cover the explanation of our experimental design using the methods described in this chapter.

Chapter 4

Experimental Design

To answer our research questions, we conducted six different kind of experiments. In the following sections, we present different types of experiments, data, research questions and evaluation.

4.1 Data and data gathering

Our data collection is a dataset of 7,502,132 classifieds (8.8 GB of memory) which is the total number of active classifieds in the period of 1 month in the site of Marktplaats. Also, we remove classifieds that are suspended from the system as being duplicates. We choose 100 classifieds from the entire data collection to represent the previously visited classifieds, thus the user's information need or topic. The classifieds were uniformly formatted into a Standard Generalized Markup Language (SGML) structure with tags for each part of a classified, as can be seen in the listing 4.1.

Listing 4.1: SGML formated classified

```
<DOC>
 <DOCNO>244563422</DOCNO>
  <TITLE>
   koop huur rietgedekte villa landhuis praktijkruimte eerbeek
  </TITLE>
  <DESCRIPTION>
   aangeboden exclusief rietgedekt modern landhuis eerbeek
      praktijkruimte eigen ingang koopprijs 998 000 kk
      huurprijs 3 300 per maand
  </DESCRIPTION>
  <CATEGORY>
   huizen en kamers huizen te koop huizen koop
  </CATEGORY>
  <PRICE>
    998.000
  </PRICE>
  <ATTRIBUTES>
   Aantal kamers 5 kamers of meer Woonoppervlakte 150 m of
      meer
  </ATTRIBUTES>
</DOC>
```

Indri search engine requires the SGML format. All classifieds have begin-
ning, end markers and unique document number (DOCNO) field. Also, they
consist of a title, a description, a price, a category and several attributes.

With the use of Indri build Index application we build repositories from the
document collection. The buildIndex application uses parameter files to create
repositories of indexes of all the classifieds (see listing 4.2).

Listing 4.2: Build index parameter file

```
<parameters>
 <index>/home/varvara/workspace/externalSources/
    indri/repositories2/mergedOutput24</index>
  <memory>1G</memory>
  <corpus>
    <path>/home/lemur/testdata/firstCorpus</path>
    <class>trectext</class>
  </corpus>
  <stemmer><name>krovetz</name></stemmer>
  <field>
    <name>p</name>
  </field>
</parameters>
```

It is necessary for our data collection to be stored contiguously on disk for optimum retrieval performance [12]. We merged the 125 repositories in six repositories with the use of dumpIndex application to improve performance. Statistics for each repository of unstemmed data collection you can find in table 4.1 and stemmed in table 4.2.

Table 4.1: Statistics of five unstemmed repositories (Rep1, Rep2, Rep3, Rep4 and Rep5). Total number of documents, unique terms and total terms for each repository is given.

	Rep1	Rep2	Rep3	Rep4	Rep5
Documents	1,440,000	1,403,211	1,440,000	1,440,000	1,440,000
Unique terms	1,126,145	1,138,034	1,135,226	1,057,184	1,066,359
Total Terms	76,223,460	67,441,399	68,602,942	68,034,636	68,206,373

Table 4.2: Statistics of five stemmed repositories (Rep1, Rep2, Rep3, Rep4 and Rep5). Total number of documents, unique terms and total terms for each repository is given.

	Rep1	Rep2	Rep3	Rep4	Rep5
Documents	1,440,000	1,403,211	1,440,000	1,440,000	1,440,000
Unique terms	1,074,828	1,081,013	1,079,051	1,006,485	1,016,282
Total Terms	76,184,789	67,405,711	68,567,148	68,002,150	68,173,834

4.2 Retrieving classifieds list

Having indexes of the document collection described above, the next step is to create an Indri-style query file like listing 4.3.

Listing 4.3: Query parameter file

```
<parameters>
 <index>/home/repositories/rep1</index>
  <query>
  <text> koop huur rietgedekte villa </text>
  <number> 244 </number>
  </query>
  <baseline>tf.idf,k1:1.0,b:0.3</baseline>
  <count>30</count>
  <trecFormat>true</trecFormat>
</parameters>
```

From the 100 chosen classifieds, we create queries in Indri-style query files like in listing 4.3. Also, creating the query involves parsing the visited classified which we use as topic to find relevant classifieds. Parsing has to be the same as the preprocessing of the document collection. Otherwise the accuracy of results will be affected negatively and the results will not be optimal. For example, if we have a query term 'books' then it will be difficult to find documents related to 'book'.

Next, the query file runs against our repositories using IndriRunQuery and retrieves the relevant list of classifieds. The output of the IndriRunQuery is a TREC style file called qrels consist of relevant classifieds to a query. These files are then input to trec_eval, to calculate the precision in five first results.

The different query models we use are the following:

. Title words

. Title and description words (unstructured data)

. Attributes and Category (structure data)

. Structure data and unstructured data

. LLR in Title words

. LLR in Title and description words

. LLR in Structure data and in unstructured data

Different retrieval systems are used for experimentation purposes. As it is mentioned in section 3.4 , our three retrieval models are:

. Tf.Idf

. Okapi BM25

. LM

4.3   Our baseline

The title of the classified is the summary of the classified. It's brief and consists of the most important information. For this reason, we use the title query model as baseline with okapi BM25 as retrieval strategy without stemming. We choose okapi which is proven that is a state of the art retrieval strategy and it performs better in our experiments in the comparison with the other two (LM, TfIdf). We are not using stemming because it harms our retrieval effectiveness as it is proven from our experiments.

4.4   Experiments

4.4.1   Query modeling

With this kind of experiment, we answer the first research question. For each of the three types of query models (classifieds' structure, discriminative terms, pseudo relevance feedback) we construct queries and submit them to our index of classifieds. We measure the performance of each system and we compare the results to evaluate the differences in performance between the models.

To create a good query model, the query has to contain the most important information from the classified. But how can we find words that contribute the most important information from a classified? In the case of classifieds we have several fields that important information can be found. Also, a lot of noise exists in the fields which harms the retrieval efficiency. Discriminative terms can be extracted by the classifieds fields. Furthermore, we can get feedback from the result lists and create new queries to improve our retrieval performance.

As a first step, we conducted an experiment to answer the first research question using query models with classified fields terms. We compare the precision of the resulted classified lists with our baseline's precision.

Furthermore we make experiments using discriminative terms and pseudo relevance feedback that are presented in the following sections.

Query models with discriminative terms   As it is described in the methodology chapter, we will use the LLR to create queries with discriminative terms. We use LLR to extract discriminative terms from the title and the entire classified. Given the visited classified field or all fields as null corpora and the big dataset of 8.8 GB classifieds as normative corpora we will produce our queries.

Query models with pseudo relevance feedback   The method we follow in order to use pseudo relevance feedback is the same method used in normal retrieval. The system will use the results from the original query and extend it with the feedback. The system assumes that the top five ranked documents are relevant. It extracts the five most frequent terms in this top five ads, expands the query with this terms and finally retrieves results with the expanded query.

4.4.2   Retrieval model

We conduct this experiment to investigate which of the three retrieval models (Okapi BM25, TfIdf, LM) is performing best (second research question). All the query models available are part of the experiment. The three retrieval methods are already described in the methodology chapter.

4.4.3   Late data fusion

With the late data fusion experiments, we give answers to the third research question. We use late fusion techniques to fuse the individual models from the query modeling experiments and we produce new result lists. Then we compare their performance in contrast with individual models.

We experiment with eight fusion techniques as explained in the methodology chapter. The results were compared with the individual models to answer the relevant research question. Since we don't have any weight in the queries, we use the MAP as a weight of a sample of classified runs. So we choose 50 random visited classifieds and we use the MAP of the trec results run. Then, we use the MAP as the weight to the WCombSUM, WcombMNZ and WcombWW methods.

4.4.4 Diversification

To answer the fourth, fifth and sixth research question, we diversify first the query models from the first experiment with MMR method. Then, we diversify with our three diversity methods explained in method section. To evaluate the results, we compare them with the MMR method.

To evaluate these experiments we used the clicks logs evaluation method described below. The assessors evaluation is based one the assumption that we are searching relevant classifieds to the visited one. While in the case of diversification, we want more diversified results in case that we will increase the possibilities that will cover the information need of the user. Clicks indicate user's interest.

In the following paragraphs, we are presenting the experimental design of the three alternative diversification methods.

MMRalt1 The algorithm of this diversification method is provided in methodology chapter. It is based on the assumption that we don't want to show two similar results in a row. So, we are taking into account only the similarity between the previous selected classified and the unselected classifieds.

MMRalt2 The algorithm of this diversification method is provided in methodology chapter. The difference with the MMR implementation is that we are calculating the average similarity for each classified with all the selected classifieds.

MMRaltAvgLst4 To answer the sixth research question we implement the algorithm provided in methodology and we compared the results with MMR. This algorithm aim to create a diverisfified sets of four classiifieds instead of taking into account the diversity between all classifieds.

Since we were doing the experiments in an industrial environment, their decisions or experience affect our decision in some cases. They wanted to expose only five results as similar classifieds paginated. This creates the idea to use windows on comparison of similarity. So the basic idea is that we want to show 5 diversified results per page. We compare only the similarity of the not selected classifieds and the previous four displayed classifieds. The algorithm we use to implement is provided on methodology chapter.

4.4.5 Data fusion of diversified result

For the last experiment, using the same late fusion techniques as in the previous experiment, we merge the diversified result lists to answer the seventh research question. We measure the difference in performance comparing the new result lists with the fused results from the previous experiments. The evaluation of the results is based on the click log evaluation as well due to the reasons mentioned in the previous section.

4.5 Evaluation

To evaluate our results and answer the research questions, we need to know which documents are relevant and if they are retrieved by the specific system. We follow two ways of evaluation. One method is using editorial ground truth and the other one is using click logs.

Editorial evaluation   In this kind of evaluation, three assessors are provided with 100 topics which in our case are the contents of the visited classifieds and they evaluate a ranked list of documents (results of each system). They judge documents as relevant or not.

The three components of a test collection are the document set, a set of information need statements called topics, and the relevance judgments that indicate which documents should be retrieved in response to a given topic. Of these three components the relevance judgments are the most expensive to produce [14]. Within big document collections, judging all documents as relevant or not is almost impossible due to the time it requires. Also based on [18] the greater the ranked position of a relevant document (of any relevance level) the less valuable it is for the user, because the less likely it is that the user will examine the document. It would therefore be desirable from the assessor viewpoint highly relevant documents to be ranked higher in the retrieval results lists.

With the use of pooling we can judge only a subset of the results. In pooling, a set of documents to be judged for a topic (the 'pool') is constructed by taking the union of the top λ documents retrieved for the topic by a variety of different retrieval methods. Each document in the pool for a topic is judged for relevance, and documents not in the pool are assumed to be irrelevant to that topic. Sakai and Mitamura [16] report the outcome of their experiment to investigate the effect of reducing both the topic set size and the pool depth and they prove that using 100 topics with depth-30 pools generally yields fewer errors than using 30 topics with depth-100 pools. For this reason, we choose to have 100 topics with depth -30 pools.

Due to the fact that different persons have different opinions about the relevance for the same document we decide to use four assessors with different background (two developers, one business analyst and a product owner). However, based on [20], multiple assessors make errors which affect the assessment. Basically the reasons lie in the ambiguity of data or mistakes of annotators due to lack of motivation or knowledge. Also, non-expert assessors judging domain-specific queries make significant errors affecting system evaluation. When assessors are not closely managed or highly trained, mistakes must be common. For this reason we calculate the kappa coefficient (K) to check the reliability of judgments. The kappa coefficient (K) measures pairwise agreement among a set of assessors making binary judgments, correcting for expected chance agreement:

$$K = P(A) - \frac{P(E)}{1 - P(E)} \tag{4.1}$$

where P(A) is the proportion of times that the assessors agree and P(E) is the proportion of times that we would expect them to agree by chance, calculated along the lines of the intuitive argument presented above [21].

In the following table we present the annotation agreement between our assessors:

Table 4.3: Inter annotator agreement between different assessors (developer a, developer b, business analyst and product owner). Proportion of times assessor agree on relevance (P(agree-rel)), proportion of times assessor agree on irrelevance (P(agree-irr)), dataset and k-measure.

Assessor a	Assessor b	DataSet	P(agree-rel)	P(agree-irr)	k-measure
Developer a	Business analyst	1,261	0.13	0.39	0.64
Developer a	Product owner	2,148	0.25	0.24	0.57
Developer a	Developer b	574	0.22	0.27	0.57
Business analyst	Product owner	820	0.23	0.26	0.54
Developer b	Product owner	574	0.15	0.37	0.52

With the previous in mind, we take the following decisions:

. To evaluate if a document is relevant or not we need the opinion of potential users of our system.

. Assessors have to be Dutch speakers. Since my document collection is in Dutch, assessors must be native Dutch speakers as well. The understanding of the language has to be appropriate to understand entirely the contents of the document.

. We use as assessors experts with different background in order to cover different kinds of users.

. Assessors without any intentions for the project. We need unbiased answers on relevance.

. Binary value for judgment: zero for irrelevant and one for relevant documents.

. Assessor will see a list of relevant documents. However, this list will be unordered because we don't want to direct assessor's opinion about relevance.

Clicks logs evaluation   In this approach, we use click logs as an indication of relevance instead of the assessors judgment. Provided with click logs of four days, we create a relevant list of all the classifieds users visited in one session after the visited classified. More into details, we create a list with all the classifieds visited after the one of the 100 classifieds we choose to see as topic. Then, we count as relevant only the classifieds which more than five different users click on it. We did the same for all 100 topic classifieds.

4.5.1 Measures

TREC is an annual conference started in 1992 co-sponsored and masterminded by the US National Institute of Standards and Technology (NIST), but tracks are largely organized by the participant research groups. It has contributed to many advances in information retrieval techniques such as ranking algorithms, improving old ideas and encouraging new ideas and experimentation.

TREC_EVAL is a tool designed for evaluation of various information retrieval systems. It handles collection of documents, queries, and relevance judgments. It takes two documents as input and it calculates various measures for retrieval system evaluation. The measure we are interested in is the precision at first five documents which is more important for similar classifieds.

Since, the experimental design of each experiment, the data we use and how we evaluate the experiments are explained, we can present the results of the experiments we conducted in the following chapter.

Chapter 5

Results

In the following sections, the experiment results are presented and analyzed. Further analysis is provided in the following chapter. The sections are separated based on the experiments that had already described in the previous chapters.

5.1 Query modeling

To answer the first research question about the best query model to improve the performance of our baseline, we conduct the query modeling experiment as it is described in the experimental design chapter. The results of this experiment are presented at the table 5.1.

Table 5.1: System performance using precision at first five results measure (P@5) of title (T), title and description (T+D), all the fields (T+D+A+C) and attribute and categories (A+C) query models using three retrieval strategies (BM25, LM, TfIdf) and two types of ground truth (editorial and click logs).

Query model	Editorial			Click logs		
	BM25	LM	TfIdf	BM25	LM	TfIdf
T	0.6560	0.5980	0.626	0.1680	0.1660	0.1540
T+D	0.6660	0.5880	0.6500	0.1700	0.1680	**0.1600**
T+D+A+C	**0.7300**	**0.6460**	**0.6860**	**0.1720**	**0.1700**	0.1580
A+C	0.4800	0.3400	0.4500	0.0920	0.0900	0.0600

The table 5.1 represents the precision at five first results from four different query models. First, we are adding fields to our baseline to see if any improvement occurs. The last query model with only attributes and category is an extra

35

query model to investigate if it consists of enough information to improve the precision of our baseline.

In the results with the editorial evaluation, adding the description to our baseline shows an improvement on precision using BM25 and TfIdf, except LM that shows a minor decrease. Adding the attributes and category gives a boost to all retrieval strategies. However, precision of query model with attributes and category is worse than our baseline's precision.

The results using the click logs evaluation indicate a slight increase in the precision when the description is used in the query models. Also, adding the attributes and category, shows a small increase but not on TfIdf. However, the attributes and category alone in the query model are not performing better than the baseline.

The results verify our initial assumption that adding extra information on the title query model can improve the performance. We can give an initial answer before further analysis to the first research question that using all the fields on the query model indicates the highest precision thus is the best one of the available query models.

5.2   Retrieval modeling

Second research question that we are answering is about the best retrieval method from the three available (Okapi BM25F, TfIdf and LM). In the table 5.1, we can compare the difference in precision bettween different retrieval methods and same query models. Furthermore, on table 5.2 we present the increase in precision using BM25F over LM and the difference in precision using BM25F over TfIdf.

Table 5.2: Percentage increase on presicion % increase of presision using BM25 instead of LM and increase of presision using BM25 instead of TfIdf. Query models used are title (T), title and description (T+D), all the fields (T+D+A+C) and attribute and categories (A+C) query models two types of ground truth (editorial and click logs).

Query model	Editorial		Click logs	
	% BM25 over LM	% BM25 over TfIdf	% BM25 over LM	% BM25 over TfIdf
T	9.7	4.8	1.2	9.1
T+D	13.3	2.5	1.2	6.2
T+D+A+C	13	6.4	1.2	8.9
A+C	41.2	6.7	2.2	53.3

In the results of the table 5.1 with editorial evaluation, LM has the smallest precision in a comparison with the other two. Systems are using BM25F increase the precision of systems using LM at least 13% using editorial evaluation and at least 1,2% using click logs evaluation. Incerase on precision on systems using BM25F over the systems using TfIdf is at least 2.5% using editorial evaluation and 6.2% using click logs evaluation. Furthermore, in results with click logs evaluation in one query model LM and TfIdf have the same precision. However, in attributes and category query models TfIdf has lower precision than LM.

Provided with the previous results, we can verify that Okapi BM25 is the retrieval strategy which performs better than the other two.

However, is important to mention here that retrieval methods are using smooth parameters that we didn't experimented with them. The assumptions we are making in this section are based on the default parameters and experimenting with them might give different results thus further investigation is needed.

5.3 Late data fusion

Different late data fusion techniques used to answer the third research question about improving the performance of the individual systems using these techniques.

Table 5.3: System performance using precision at first five results measure (P@5) of late data fusion methods (combMAX, combMIN, combSUM, combMNZ, combANZ, WcombSUM, WcomMNZ, WcombWW) and the best individual system using two types of ground truth (editorial and click logs).

	Editorial	Clicks logs
Best individual	**0.7300**	0.1720
combMAX	0.5400	0.1280
combMIN	0.0760	0.0020
combSUM	0.6160	0.1720
combMNZ	0.6460	0.1720
combANZ	0.0800	0.0020
WcombSUM	0.6140	**0.1740**
WcombMNZ	0.6360	**0.1740**
WcombWW	0.6320	**0.1740**

The table 5.3 represents all the late fusion methods we use to answer the third research question in a comparison with the individual best system. The most important observation of this table is that none of the fused systems is performing better than the individual one using the editorial evaluation.

On the results with the editorial evaluation, the combMNZ is performing better than the rest of the fused systems. The rest of the fused systems have small differences in the precision except of the combMIN and combANZ that have very low precision.

On the results with click logs evaluation, the weighted fused systems have better precision than the rest. Then, a slight decrease in precision is seen on combMNZ and combMAX and a bigger decrease on combMAX. Same as editorial evaluation, the combANZ and combMIN have the lowest precision.

5.4   Diversification

In this set of experiments we answer the following research questions:
The research questions we aim to answer are the following:

1. Are the results of diversification affected if only the similarity with the previous displayed classified is taken into account?

2. Are the results of diversification affected if the average similarity of previous displayed docs is taken into account?

3. Are the results of diversification affected if only the similarity with the previous four displayed classifieds is taken into account?

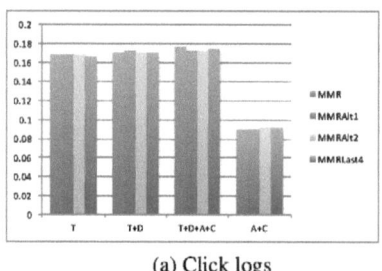
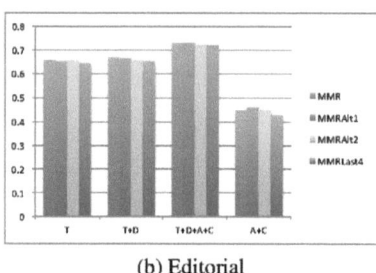

(a) Click logs   (b) Editorial

Figure 5.1: Bar graphs with the system performance (P@5) of diversification methods MMR, MMRAlt1, MMRAlt2, MMRLast4 using title (T), title and description (T+D), all the fields (T+D+A+C) and attribute and categories (A+C) query models and two types of ground truth (editorial and click logs).

In the figure 5.1, the precision at five first results for the diversification methods using four different query models is presented. In both graphs the trends are almost the same thus none of the systems performs better than the others. So, as a first conclusion that can make with regard to the diversification research questions (four, five and six) is that none of which performs better than the MMR method proposed on [26].

5.5 Fused diversified results

The final research question is weather fusing diversified ranked lists improves the performance of the not diversified systems.

Table 5.4: System performance using precision at first five results measure (P@5) of late data fusion methods (combMAX, combMIN, combSUM, combMNZ, combANZ, WcombSUM, WcombMNZ, WcombWW) of fused system and fused diversified system using two types of ground truth (editorial and click logs). Also, percentage increase from fused diversified results over the fused not diversified (% IOD) is provided for both ground truths.

	Editorial			Click logs		
	Fused diversified	Fused not diversified	% increase	Fused diversified	Fused not diversified	% increase
combMAX	**0.7320**	0.5400	35.5%	0.1700	0.1280	32.8
combMIN	0.0800	0.0760	5.3	0.0020	0.0020	0
combSUM	0.6700	0.6160	8.8	0.1720	0.1720	0
combMNZ	0.6700	0.6460	3.7	0.1720	0.1720	0
combANZ	0.0940	0.0800	17.5	0.0040	0.0020	100
WcombSUM	0.6620	0.6140	7.8	0.1720	**0.1740**	-1.15
WcombMNZ	0.6560	0.6360	3.1	0.1720	**0.1740**	-1.15
WcombWW	0.6560	0.6320	3.8	0.1720	**0.1740**	-1.15

The table 5.4 represents the comparison of the fused diversified systems versus the fused individual systems with both click logs and editorial evaluation to answer this reasearch question.

Using the click logs evaluation, we can see that the precision of combANZ is doubled when we fuse the diversified instead of fuse the not diversified ranked lists. Also, the precision increased by 32.8% on combMAX fusion of diverified system over the combMAX fusion of not diversified systems. The rest of the fusion methods either they don't have any improvement or they even have decrease in acomparison of the fusion of diversified systems with the fusion of not diversified.

Using editorial evaluation show us an improvement on the precision when the diversified lists are fused. Also, the biggest difference is in the combMAX which has an increase of 0.19. The smallest increase we have in table 5.4 is the combANZ which is 0.014. Also, combMAX fusion of diversified ranked lists outperforms even our best individual system (T+D+A+D) using BM25F by 11.6%.

Further measurements of data fusion of all the proposed diversification methods can be seen on 8.13, 8.14, 8.15, 8.16.

In sum, using the editorial evaluation we can verify and answer to the seventh research question that the fused diversified systems perform better than the fused not diversified systems. Using the click log evaluation, we can not give the same answer cause the results in the table don't show any large improvement.

Our research questions have already been answered with the results of this chapter. A deeper analysis and assumptions about the reasons we have these results are provided in the next chapter.

Chapter 6

Analysis

We provide a further analysis about the results of the experiments described in the previous chapter. We also present our initial assumptions about each experiment and we are presenting extra experiments conducted in order to prove them.

6.1 Stemming experiment

Preprocessing is a good approach to improve the effectiveness of retrieval systems. The document collection consists of classifieds created by regular users and contains a lot of noise which should be extracted before indexing takes place. Removing the noise can improve query efficiency. Thus, we hypothesize that using stemming will retrieve more relevant results. For example, "cars" will be stemmed in "car". If we have a document related to "car", it will be retrieved as well.

We make one initial experiment to measure if any change on performance occurs when we use stemming in the preprocessing phase. In this phase we use two different query models and we compare the results with stemming used in the preprocessing and without.

We preprocess the document collection and we convert it in lowercase, remove stopwords, replace punctuations with spaces and remove words with one or two characters. Also, for experimentation purposes we compare two approaches (with or without stemming). Stemming is based on the snowball stemmer. Then, the data saved in SGML formatted documents.

Table 6.1: System performance using precision at first five results measure (P@5) of title (T), title using LLR (T-LLR) query models with and without stemming using three retrieval strategies (BM25, LM, TfIdf) and two types of ground truth (editorial and click logs).

	Editorial			Click logs		
	BM25	LM	TfIdf	BM25	LM	TfIdf
T	**0.6560**	0.5980	0.626	**0.1680**	0.1660	0.1540
T-stemming	0.6040	0.5660	0.5640	0.1640	0.1660	0.1600
T-LLR	**0.5660**	0.5160	0.5280	**0.1580**	0.1540	0.1500
T-stemming-LLR	0.5280	0.5160	0.4980	**0.1580**	0.1560	0.1460

Based on the results on table 6.1 using editorial evaluation, stemming decrease the precision at least 0.3 and the maximum of 0.5 at Okapi BM25. There is no difference in precision in the query model with LLR on title field using LM. Based on the results using click logs evaluation, there is no big decrease in the results with stemming but neither an improvement. The only case that a small increase in performance happened is on the title query using TFIDF.

We believe that the reason of the previous results is that stemming negatively affects the queries accuracy. For instance, if we search for "organization" and our stemmer removes the reasonably common suffix "ization" we end up with classifieds about "organ". Also, we found examples that didn't retrieve any relevant classifieds on the first five results, while there were at least two relevant results in the systems without stemming. Also, we observe that the same classifieds in the result list have lower score due to the fact that the frequency of stemmed terms are greater.

For further analysis, we are presenting the results of the table 6.2 with relevant results retrieved only when stemming is used and the relevant results retrieved only without stemming. We take into account the ranked classified list of title query model using BM25 without stemming and the ranked classified list of the title query model BM25 using stemming. We gather all the relevant retrieved classifieds by only one of the two systems. Then we group them by topic and we count the total number of topics retrieved one relevant classified on the top five classified that is not retrieved by the other system. Then, we count the total number of topics retrieved two classifieds are not retrieved by the other system etc. We take into account only the top 5 results. For example we present that 31 topics retrieved 1 relevant classified by the system using title query model and BM25 without stemming that is not retrieved by the other system using stemming.

Table 6.2: Number of relevant classifieds retrieved on the top five results, number of examples retrieve uniquely this number of classifieds with title query model (T) and BM25 without stemming, number of examples retrieve uniquely this number of classifieds with title query model and BM25 with stemming (T-stemming).

Relevant classifieds	T	T-stemming
1	31	26
2	12	5
3	3	2
4	1	0

The uniquely retrieved results from the non stemmed system are more than the uniquely retrieved by the stemmed system. There are 31 topics that retrieve one unique relevant classified that is not retrieved in the first 5 results of the stemmed systems. Also, there are 16 visited classifieds retrieved more than one unique relevant classified that is not retrieved in the first five results of the stemmed systems. However, this not a strong indication, we decide not to use stemming in the rest of the experiments since none of the systems using stemming improve the performance of our baseline.

6.2 Query modeling

We hypothesize that combining all the classifieds fields in our baseline, we will improve the precision of the five first results. In the results provided in the table 5.1 this assumption is proved. Adding the description in the baseline's query model improved the performance. Furthermore, adding the attributes and category had the best precision in all three retrieval strategies using either editorial evaluation or click log evaluation.

Also, during the assembly of our editorial evaluation we observed the following:

. In some classifieds like men/women shoes, there is no difference in the text of the classifieds except of the category name. Thus, queries like title and description do not perform as well as query models including the category name.

. Also in the same case, attributes will add extra value due to the extra information about the size and the kind of shoe.

. Classifieds related to products as topic had as result classifieds the parts for this product. However, the parts of the product is not always relevant to the product.

To further analyze the results we are presenting the table 6.3 with the extra relevant results retrieved when description is added on the query model. We used the title and description query model using BM25 and our baseline. The construction of the table is with the same way the table 6.2 is constructed.

Table 6.3: Number of relevant classifieds retrieved on the top five results, number of examples retrieve uniquely this number of classifieds with title and description query model and BM25 (T+D), number of examples retrieve uniquely this number of classifieds with title query model and BM25 (T).

Relevant classifieds	T+D	T
1	15	26
2	12	11
3	13	3
4	4	1

As you can see, the query model with title and description has a lot of relevant results retrieved while they are not retrieved from title query model. Although there are much more cases that only one relevant result retrieved uniquely from only title query (26 versus 15), the number of the rest of the cases (that more than one uniquely retrieved from the description and title query model) outperform it e.g 13 versus 3. In total 44 relevant classifieds uniquely retrieved from title and description query model and 41 from title query model.

Furthermore, we are presenting the table 6.4 with the uniquely relevant results retrieved when all the fields are in the query model in a comparison with the description query model. The construction of the table is with the same way the table 6.2 is constructed.

Table 6.4: Number of relevant classifieds retrieved on the top five results, number of examples retrieve uniquely this number of classifieds with all fields in query model and BM25 (T+D+A+C), number of examples retrieve uniquely this number of classifieds with title and description query model and BM25 (T+D).

Relevant classifieds	T+D+A+C	T+D
1	39	28
2	18	18
3	8	5
4	6	3
5	1	1

As you can see from the table 6.4, 72 uniquely retrieved results from all the fields query model and 55 from title and description query model. Furthermore, the uniquely retrieved results from all the fields are more or equal than description query model. Moreover, in table 6.5, we can see that 219 classifieds are retrieved by both query models. Title query model retrieved 109 relevant results are not retrieved on the entire query model while entire retrieved 146, That's a good indication that, the extra information on the attributes and category improves the results due to the fact that more relevant classifieds retrieved.

Table 6.5: Number of relevant classifieds retrieved by title (T), all fields (T+D+A+C) query model and number of common retrieved relevant classifieds.

Query model	Total number
T	328
T+D+A+C	365
Common	219

Also, we are presenting the table 6.6 with the uniquely relevant results retrieved when all the fields are in the query model in a comparison with the baseline. The construction of the table is with the same way the table 6.2 is constructed.

Table 6.6: Number of relevant classifieds retrieved on the top five results, number of examples retrieve uniquely this number of classifieds with all fields in query model and BM25 (T+D+A+C), number of examples retrieve uniquely this number of classifieds with title query model and BM25 (T).

Relevant classifieds	T+D+A+C	T
1	37	22
2	16	19
3	12	8
4	9	5
5	1	1

The uniquely retrieved results from all the fields are more or equal than our baseline except of the case that 2 unique results are retrieved in the top five results. In total, 75 uniquely retrieved results from all the fields query model and 55 from title query model. Furthermore, in table 8.1, we present more measures for all the query models that proves the same assumptions. Precision at first ten results is increased when title is added to the baseline and has the best score when attributes and category added as well. Also, similar observations we had using MAP or Rprec as measurements. However, in 8.2, the results are not so clear but they they don't disprove our initial assumptions.

We also observed that query model with attributes and category indicates the lowest precision in a comparison with the rest of the query models. We hypothesize that not enough information exists to attributes and category, thus the results will be negative. To further prove that assumption, we are presenting the table 6.7 with the uniquely relevant results retrieved when attributes and category are only in the query model in a comparison with the baseline. The construction of the table is with the same way the table 6.2 is constructed.

Table 6.7: Number of relevant classifieds retrieved on the top five results, number of examples retrieve uniquely this number of classifieds with attributes and category in query model and BM25 (A+C), number of examples retrieve uniquely this number of classifieds with title query model and BM25 (T).

Relevant classifieds	A+C	T
1	16	17
2	12	16
3	16	18
4	16	29
5	5	9

It is obvious in the previous results that query model with only attribute and category has less uniquely retrieved results than our baseline. Also, in the results chapter the query model using only attributes and category has the lowest precision, thus we can conclude that attributes and category alone are not containing enough information to improve the precision of query with title.

Query models with discriminative terms Our assumption was that discriminative terms will retrieve less results but more accurate due to the fact that a more accurate query is created. Thus, the precision at first five will be increased. To prove this assumption, we present the results of the table 6.8 with the six different systems.

Table 6.8: System performance using precision at first five results measure (P@5) of title (T), title using LLR (T-LLR), title using stemming (T-stemming), title using both LLR and stemming (T-LLR stemming), all fields (T+D+A+C) and all fields using LLR (T+D+A+C-LLR) query models and two types of ground truth (editorial and click logs).

	Editorial			Click logs		
	BM25	LM	TfIdf	BM25	LM	TfIdf
T	**0.6560**	0.5980	0.626	**0.1680**	0.1660	0.1540
T-LLR	0.5660	0.5160	0.5280	0.1580	0.1540	0.1500
T-stemming	**0.6040**	0.5660	0.5640	0.1640	**0.1660**	0.1600
T-stemming-LLR	0.5280	0.5160	0.4980	0.1580	0.1560	0.1460
T+D+A+C	**0.7300**	0.6460	0.6860	**0.1720**	0.1700	0.1580
T+D+A+C-LLR	0.6360	0.5400	0.5740	0.1600	0.1640	0.1540

Based on the results, all the systems are negatively affected in a comparison with the systems with the discriminative terms. Using the editorial evaluation, big decrease from all the fields query model to LLR all the fields query model in all three retrieval strategies is indicated. Smaller decreases in the rest of the systems are shown but none of them show any improvement. Since using stemming and relevance in the title query hurts the performance even more than 0.10, we decided not to use it in the rest of the query models.

We hypothesize that the reason of the previous results is that LLR is removing some important information thus relevant results are not retrieved. To prove that, we are presenting the table 6.9 with the count of relevant results retrieved only when LLR is used in a system and the count of relevant results retrieved only in the same system without the use of LLR. The construction of the table is with the same way the table 6.2 is constructed.

Table 6.9: Number of relevant classifieds retrieved on the top five results, number of examples retrieve uniquely this number of classifieds with LLR and all fields query model (T+D+A+C-LLR) in the query model and BM25, number of examples retrieve uniquely this number of classifieds with all fields query model (T+D+A+C) and BM25.

Relevant classifieds	T+D+A+C-LLR	T+D+A+C
1	39	38
2	10	12
3	2	1

No obvious difference is observed in table 6.9 thus this subject will be added on the future work due to time constraint. One possible explanation that precision is harmed is that the the same relevant classifieds are scored less when LLR is used due to less word matching. Thus, they retrieve the same relevant classifieds but with different rank.

Query models with pseudo relevance feedback

Pseudo relevance feedback extends the query and more relevant classifieds retrieved. To prove this assumption, we analyze the results of the table 6.10 with two different systems.

Table 6.10: System performance using precision at first five results measure (P@5) of all fields (T+D+A+C) and all fields using pseudo relevance feedback (T+D+A+C-Pseudo) query models and two types of ground truth (editorial and click logs).

	Editorial			Click logs		
	BM25	LM	TfIdf	BM25	LM	TfIdf
T+D+A+C	**0.7300**	0.6460	0.6860	**0.1720**	0.1700	0.1580
Pseudo(T+D+A+C)	**0.7300**	0.4920	0.6520	**0.1720**	0.1620	0.1500

The results of the table 6.10 show that in the case of LM and TfIdf there is a decrease in the P@5, but in the case of Okapi it remains stable. Since the pseudo relevance feedback is an expensive procedure due to the fact that it needs to retrieve results, take feedback and then to retrieve new result list, we decide that we will not use pseudo relevance feedback on the rest of the query models.

6.3 Retrieval methods

In the results provided in results chapter, we can see that Okapi BM25 performs better than the other two. In the following table we further prove the same assumption. We present the count of relevant and irrelevant results retrieved of each retrieval strategy.

Table 6.11: Retrieval strategies (BM25, LM, TfIdf), count of relevant results and count of irrelevant results retrieved from each one.

	Relevant	Irrelevant
BM25	**3121**	1879
LM	2399	2101
TfIdf	2633	**1858**

It is obvious that Okapi BM25 retrieves the biggest number of relevant results. Though, TfIdf retrieves 21 less irrelevant results. However, the fact that the precision of Okapi BM25 is always the greatest in all query models, makes us enough confident to say that Okapi BM25 is better than the other two.

6.4 Late data fusion

In the results using editorial evaluation of table 5.3, we can see that late data fusion methods are not performing better than the best individual system. We were expecting that combMIN will have the worst precision since it takes into account the smallest score. But, we believed that combMNZ will perform better than the best individual system due to the fact that it boosts score and rank of a relevant classified that is agreed upon many systems.

From the other side, using the click logs evaluation the precision is improved on the weighted fusion methods (WcombSUM, WcombMNZ, WcombWW), but the difference is just 0.02 which is not enough to make us confident to say that they perform better. Our assumption is that we have these results because we fused all the systems together. Some of the systems are not performing as well as others and this needs further investigation to be proved.

For future work further analysis, more measures results are presented on 8.3 using three retrieval models and two ground truth types (editorial and click logs).

In an attempt to improve these results, we conduct one extra experiment with combANZ keeping stable all systemic differences i.e. stemming, query modeling but retrieval strategy. We compare the results with combANZ result from the fusion of all individual systems to see if any improvement occurs. We choose to improve combANZ fusion as an example. In future investigation the rest of the fusion methods can be used in the same way.

Table 6.12: Systems used on the combANZ with stable systemic differences are presented. Explanation is given for the use of fields use in the query model, log likelihood ratio (LLR), stemming and pseudo relevance feedback (PRF).

Name	Fields	Stemming	LLR	PRF
T	title	no	no	no
T-LLR	title	no	yes	no
T stemming	title	yes	no	no
T-LLR stemming	title	yes	yes	no
T+D	title, description	no	no	no
T+D+A+C	title, description, category, attributes	no	no	no
A+C	attributes, category	no	no	no
T+D+A+C-LLR	title, description, category, attributes	no	yes	no
T+D+A+C-Pseudo	title, description, category, attributes	no	no	yes

Table 6.13: System performance using precision at first five results measure (P@5) of combANZ keeping stable systemic differences in a comparison with combANZ merged from all systems using editorial and click logs evaluation. Query models used are title (T), title using LLR (T-LLR), title using stemming (T-stemming), title and description (T+D), all the fields (T+D+A+C) and attribute and categories (A+C), all the fields using LLR (T+D+A+C-LLR), all the fields using pseudo relevance feedback (T+D+A+C-pseudo) query models and two types of ground truth (editorial and click logs).

Query model	Editorial	Click logs
T	0.2740	0.0700
T-LLR	0.2600	0.0520
T stemming	0.1520	0.0180
T-LLR stemming	0.0800	0.0060
T+D	0.2660	0.0220
T+D+A+C	0.2120	0.0200
A+C	0.1600	0.0080
T+D+A+C-LLR	0.1780	0.0280
T+D+A+C-Pseudo	0.1440	0.0280
combANZ	0.0800	0.0020

As you can see in the table 6.13, the combANZ is improved when the systemic differences kept stable. However they didn't outperform the precision of the individuals (see table 5.1).

51

Furthermore, more measures results are presented in table 8.4 using three retrieval models and two ground truth types (editorial and click logs).

To conclude, the fusion of the results doesn't outperform the performance of the best individual system. However, we achieved to improve the effectiveness of combANZ when systemic differences kept stable. Thus, in the future plans, we can do the same experiment for the rest of the fusion method as well.

6.5   Diversification

As you can see in the bar graphs in the results chapter, there is no big improvement in precision using either editorial or click logs evaluation and the alternative diversification approaches. Our assumption is that our results are too diversified already. This assumption can be proved if the precision in the individual systems is the same with the diversified systems. The table 6.14 presents the results of BM25 individual systems and BM25 diversified systems using editorial evaluation and click logs evaluation.

Table 6.14: System performance using precision at first five results measure (P@5) of diversified and individual systems using title (T), title and description (T+D), all the fields (T+D+A+C) and attribute and categories (A+C) query models, okapi BM25 retrieval strategy (BM25) and two types of ground truth (editorial and click logs).

| | Editorial evaluation | | Click logs evaluation | |
	Individuals	Diversified	Individuals	Diversified
T	0.6560	0.6580	0.1680	0.1680
(T+D)	0.6660	0.6700	0.1700	0.1700
(T+D+A+C)	0.7300	0.7300	0.1720	0.1760
(A+C)	0.4800	0.4460	0.0920	0.0900

The differences in precision are really low in both evaluation approaches. We believe that the reason is that the initially retrieved results from the individual strategies are already diversified.

Further analysis for each of the alternative diversification methods is provided on the following paragraphs.

MMRalt1   The fact that the precision is not affected by this diversification approach is a positive sign. We take into account only the last one selected instead of all the previous. From the other side that can be a prove that our classifieds are enough diversified that are not affected by any diversification method.

MMRalt2   In this approach we used the average similarity in the calculation of the new score instead of choosing the maximum one. Thus, this approach can be used as an alternative since it doesn't affect the precision.

MMRaltAvgLast4   Same with the MMRalt1 approach, is a good sign that the precision is not affected by this algorithm due to the fact that we are comparing only the previous four selected results.

Further measurements and results for the rest of the retrieval models can be seen on 8.5 and 8.6 for MMR, 8.7 and 8.8 for MMRalt1, 8.9 and 8.10 for MMRalt2, 8.11 and 8.12 for MMRaltAvgLast4.

The analysis of our results gives us ideas for future work that are covered in the next chapter. The summary and conclusion of this work is provided as well.

Chapter 7

Conclusion

In the previous two chapters, we answered our research questions and we provided our contribution on each part of our approach. Ideas created for future work in each section are presented in this chapter that we summarize and conclude our work.

We presented multiple experiments to find the best performing system for retrieving similar classifieds. Similar classifieds is a list with classifieds recommended to the user based on his previous interest. We explored multiple ways to create this list by using the contents of the previous classified the user visited. We evaluated the performance of the results based on the precision which is affected by the relevant or irrelevant results that are retrieved. A company provided us with all the data we needed to implement the experiments. They also provided us assessors (persons that dudje each resulted similar classifieds list's item as rellevant or irrelevant) for the evaluation of the experiments.

We made experiments to find the best query model in a comparison with the title query model which is the one the company is already using and is considered our baseline. We investigated which is the best retrieval strategy between BM25F, LM and TfIdf. We fused all the systems to improve their precision. Furthermore, we made experiments for diversification of the results. Finally, we investigated if the fusion of the diversified results improves the precision. We evaluated our experiment results using two different indications of relevance, the editorial which was based on assessors judgment on relevance and click logs which was based on users history.

Results from the stemming experiment proved that the presicion of our baseline is decreased when we use stemming. Also, we presented a big number of relevant results that are not retrieved when stemming is used. Thus, we decided to not use it in any other query model. In future work, more investigation is needed for the reasons that stemming decreased the precision.

Experimental evidence proved that the more information we add to the query model the better the system performs. Eventually, the query model based on the entire classified content performs the best. Also, during the editorial evaluation that we examined visited classifieds and lists with similar classifieds, we observed that attributes and category add a lot of information to the query. However, when it is used alone (without the title and description terms) is not enough to cover the information need. Furthermore, the experimental results show us also that attributes and category alone in the query model is the worst performing system. In future work, the search query a user did to find the visited classified can be added in the query model as extra information to see if there is any improvement in precision. Also, change in the precision can be investigated when all the possible combinations of the fields on query modeling are used.

On an extra experiment we made, we proved that choosing discriminative terms instead of all terms of the classified is not performing as good in terms of precision. Also, there is no big difference on the amount of relevant results retrieved by the same systems using LLR or without. Thus, the difference in the precision of systems using LLR approach needs further investigation.

The results of the pseudo relevance feedback experiment, show us no improvement in the precision and we didn't use it in more query models.

On retrieval method experiments, okapi BM25 performs better than TfIdf and LM retrieval models in both types of evaluations and in all query models. Therefore, it leaves us no doubt about which is the best retrieval method to improve our systems performance.

The experimental results for late data fusion experiments proved that none of the late fusion methods improves the precision of the best individual system. However, in an attempt to analyze it further and prove the reason that the results are not as expected, we conducted an extra experiment of combANZ keeping stable the systemic differences. With this experiment we improve the compANZ performance but it was not performing better than the best individual. More experiments for the rest of the fusion methods using the same approach can be investigated in the future.

Also, we compared four diversification approaches to find the best performing one. None of them shows any difference in precision either using editorial or click logs evaluation. However, diversification is an expensive procedure due to the fact that you have to check the text similarity between all classifieds in the result list. Thus, the first alternative diversification method (MMRalt1) that compares only the previous selected classified with all the non selected, can be proved better because it doesn't affect the precision and is faster. Same is for the third alternative method (MMRaltAvgLast4) which takes into account only the previous four selected classifieds. But the assumption that these are faster and the fact that this makes them better needs a further investigation and a proper benchmark to be proved. Also, we already made the assumption that maybe the results are already diversified and that's why we don't have any big difference on the precision of the top five first results. In future work the similarity of the classifieds to prove if this assumption is true or not can be investigated.

Finally, we experiment with the fusion of the diversified results and we compare them initially with the fused individual systems. The results indicate that fusion of diversified results improves the precision. We also compare the results with the best individual system from the query model experiment and it's proved that combMAX improves even the performance of the best individual system. In future plans, these refinements can be compared with the diversification of fused results from Liang et al approach [38].

In conclusion, we improved the precision of the similar classifieds baseline's query model by 11,3% using all the classifieds fields in the query modeling and BM25F retrieval method. We also found that the precision of systems using BM25F is increased by at least 2,5% compared to systems using TfIdf. Additionally, the precision of systems using BM25F is incresed by at least 1,2% compared to systems using LM. We proved that fusion of results is not performing better than our individual best system but we did manage to improve the precision of one of the fusion methods by at least 80%. We achieved this by fusing systems with the same systemic differences but different retrieval methods. We proposed three alternative diversification methods but none of them had a big improvement in comparison with the MMR [26]. Finally, we fused the diversified results and we achieved the greatest precision which was 11,6% higher than the best individual system which was using all fields and BM25F.

Bibliography

[1] Valentin Jijkoun, Gilad Mishne, Maarten de Rijke. *Preprocessing Documents to Answer Dutch Questions*. In proceedings of the 15th belgian-dutch conference on artificial intelligence BNAIC03, pages: 487-497.

[2] Christopher D. Manning, Prabhakar Raghavan, Hinrich Schtze. *An introduction to Information Retrieval*. Cambridge University Press, July 7, 2008.

[3] Hao Yang, Shuaib Ding. *Inverted Index Compression and Query Processing with Optimized Document Ordering*. In proceedings of the 18 International conference of World wide web, WWW '09, pages: 401-410.

[4] Shouning Qu, Sujuan Wang, Yann Zou. *Improvement of Text Feature Selection Method based on TFIDF*. In proceedings of the 2008 International Seminar on Future, Information Technology and Management Engineering, FITME '08, pages: 79-81.

[5] Fang Hui, Tao Tao, Zhai Chengxiang. *Diagnostic Evaluation of Information Retrieval Models*. ACM Transactions on Information Systems (TOIS) - Special issue on research and development in information retrieval TOIS Homepage archive, July 1991, pages: 187 - 222.

[6] W. Bruce Croft, John Lafferty. *Language Modeling for Information Retrieval*. Springer Publishing Company, 2010.

[7] Chengxiang Zhai, John Lafferty. *A Study of Smoothing Methods for Language Models Applied to Ad Hoc Information Retrieval*. Proceedings of the 24th annual international ACM SIGIR conference on Research and development in information retrieval, SIGIR '01, pages: 334 - 342.

[8] Amit Singhal. *Modern Information Retrieval: a brief overview by Amit Singhal*. Bulletin of the IEEE computer society technical committee on data engineering.

[9] Paul Rayson, Roger Garside. *Comparing Corpora using Frequency Profiling*. In proceedings of the workshop on Comparing Corpora, held in conjunction ACL 2000, October 2000, Hong Kong, pages: 1-6.

[10] Wilkins Peter. *An Investigation Into Weighted Data Fusion for Content-Based Multimedia Information Retrieval*. PhD thesis, Dublin City University, Nov 2009.

[11] Christian Middleton, Ricardo Baeza-yates. *A Comparison of Open Source Search Engines*. SIGIR 2007.

[12] Trevor Strohman. *Dynamic collections in Indri*. 2005.

[13] Paul Rayson, Roger Garside. *Comparing Corpora using Frequency Profiling*. WCC '00 Proceedings of the workshop on Comparing corpora - Volume 9, pages: 1-6.

[14] Chris Buckley, Darrin Dimmick, Ian Soboroff, Ellen Voorhees. *Bias and the Limits of Pooling for Large Collections*. Information Retrieval, December 2007, pages: 491-508.

[15] Stephen Robertson. *On the history of evaluation in IR*. Journal of Information Science August 2008, pages: 439-456.

[16] Tetsuya Sakai, Teruko Mitamura. *Boiling Down Information Retrieval Test Collections*. RIAO '10 Adaptivity, Personalization and Fusion of Heterogeneous Information, France 2010, pages: 49-56.

[17] Craig Macdonald, Iadh Ounis, Ian Soboroff. *Overview of the TREC-2009 Blog Track*. In Proceedings of TREC 2009.

[18] Kalervo Jrvelin, Jaana Keklinen. *IR evaluation methods for retrieving highly relevant documents*. SIGIR '00 Proceedings of the 23rd annual international, ACM SIGIR conference on Research and development in information retrieval, pages 41-48.

[19] Tefko Saracevic. *Relevance: A Review of the Literature and a Framework for Thinking on the Notion in Information Science.Part III: Behavior and Effects of Relevance*. Proceedings of the 31st Annual International ACM SIGIR Conference on Research and Development in Information Retrieval, SIGIR 2008, Singapore, 2008, pages: 20-24.

[20] Azzah Al-Maskari, Mark Sanderson, Paul Clough. *Relevance Judgments between TREC and Non-TREC Assessors*. November 2007, pages: 2126 - 2144.

[21] Jean Carletta. *Assessing Agreement on Classification Tasks:The Kappa Statistic*. Computational Linguistics, June 1996, pages: 249-254.

[22] Donna Harman. *Overview of the First Text REtrieval Conference (TREC-1)*. National Institute of Standards and Technology, Gaithersburg, SIGIR '93 Proceedings of the 16th annual international ACM SIGIR conference on Research and development in information retrieval, pages: 36-47.

[23] Donna Harman. *Overview of the Second Text REtrieval Conference (TREC-2)*. National Institute of Standards and Technology, Gaithersburg, TREC-2 Proceedings of the second conference on Text retrieval conference archive, pages: 271-289.

[24] James P Callan, W Bruce Croft. *An Evaluation of Query Processing Strategies Using the TIPSTER Collection*. In Proceedings of the 16th annual international ACM SIGIR Conference on Research and Development in Information Retrieval.

[25] H.P. Luhn. *A statistical approach to mechanized encoding and searching of literary information*. IBM Journal Research and Development, 1957.

[26] J. Carbonell, J. Goldstein. *The use of MMR, diversity-based reranking for reordering documents and producing summaries*. In Research and Development in Information Retrieval, 1998.

[27] R. Agrawal, S. Gollapudi, A. Halverson and S. Ieong. *Diversifying search results*. Proceedings of the 16th international conference on World Wide Web, WWW '07.

[28] C. Zhai, J. Lafferty. *A Risk Minimization Framework for Information Retrieval*. Information Processing and Management: an International Journal, 2006.

[29] H. Chen, D. Karger. *Less is More-Probabilistic Models for Retrieving Fewer Relevant Documents*. In Proceedings of the ACM Conference on Research and Development in Information Retrieval, 2006.

[30] M. Drosou, E. Pitoura. *POIKILO: A Tool for Evaluating the Results of Diversification Models and Algorithms*. Proceedings of the VLDB Endowment VLDB Endowment, Volume 6 Issue 12, August 2013.

[31] P. Chandar, B.Carterette. *Analysis of Various Evaluation Measures for Diversity*. Proceedings of the 1st International Workshop on Diversity in Document Retrieval at European Conference on Information Retrieval, ECIR11.

[32] N. J. Belkin, P. Kantor, E. A. Fox, J. A. Shaw. *Combining the evidence of multiple query representations for information retrieval.* Information Processing and Management, 1995.

[33] J. H. Lee. *Analyses of Multiple Evidence Combination.* Proceedings of the 20th annual international ACM SIGIR conference on Research and development in information retrieval, SIGIR '97.

[34] A.Chowdhury, O. Frieder, D. Grossman, C. McCabe. *Analyses of Multiple-Evidence Combinations for Retrieval Strategies.* Proceedings of the 24th annual international ACM SIGIR conference on Research and development in information retrieval, SIGIR '01.

[35] S. M. Beitzel, E. C. Jensen, A. Chowdhury, O. Frieder, D. Grossman, N. Goharian. *Disproving the Fusion Hypothesis: An Analysis of Data Fusion via Effective Information Retrieval Strategies.* Proceedings of the 2003 ACM Symposium on Applied Computing.

[36] S. M. Beitzel, E. C. Jensen, A. Chowdhury, D. Grossman, O. Frieder, N. Goharian. *On fusion of effective retrieval strategies in the same information retrieval system.* Journal of the American Society of Information Science and Technology, 2004.

[37] R. Nuray, F. Can. *Automatic ranking of information retrieval using data fusion.* Information Processing and Management, 2006.

[38] S. Liang, Z. Ren, M. de Rijke. *Fusion helps diversification.* 37th international ACM SIGIR conference on Research and development in information retrieval, 2014.

[39] Abhinandan S. Das, Mayur Data, Ashutosh Garg, Shyam Rajaram. *Google news personalization: scalable online collaborative filtering.* WWW '07 Proceedings of the 16th international conference on World Wide Web, pages: 271-280.

[40] Nico Schlitter, Tanja Falkowski. *Mining the Dynamics of Music Preferences from a Social Networking Site.* Social Network Analysis and Mining, 2009. ASONAM '09. International Conference on Advances, pages: 243 - 248.

[41] Sean Owen, Robin Anil, Ted Dunning and Ellen Friedman. *Mahood in action.* Manning Publications, October 17, 2011.

[42] Eric Hatcher, Otis Cospodnetic, Michael McCandless. *Lucene in action.* Manning Publications, July 28, 2010.

[43] Raymond Kosala, Hendrik Blockeel. *Web Data Mining Research: A Survey*. Computational Intelligence and Computing Research(ICCIC), 2010 IEEE International Conference, pages: 1-10.

[44] R. K. Roul, S. K. Sahay. *An Effective Information Retrieval for Ambiguous Query*. Asian Journal of Computer Science and Information Technology, March 2012, Vol. 2 Issue 3, pages: 26.

[45] Gregory D. Linden, Jennifer A. Jacobi, Eric A. Benson. *Collaborative recommendations using item-to-item similarity mappings*. Google Patents, 2001/07/24.

[46] Balog, Krisztian and Weerkamp, Wouter and de Rijke, Maarten. *A Few Examples Go a Long Way: Constructing Query Models from Elaborate Query Formulations*. Proceedings of the 31st Annual International ACM SIGIR Conference on Research and Development in Information Retrieval, SIGIR '08, pages = 371–378,

[47] Meij and Edgar. *Combining Concepts and Language Models for Information Access*. SIGIR Forum, June 2011,

Chapter 8

Appendix

8.1 Query modeling

Table 8.1: Four measures (P5, P@10, MAP, Rpr) of title (T), title and description (T+D), all the fields (T+D+A+C) and attribute and categories (A+C) using log likelihood ratio for discriminative terms (LLR), stemming and pseudo relevance feedback(Pseudo) query models and all three retrieval strategies (BM25, TfIdf, LM) with editorial evaluation.

System	BM25				TfIdf				LM			
	P5	P10	MAP	Rpr	P5	P10	MAP	Rpr	P5	P10	MAP	Rpr
T	0.6560	0.4910	0.2821	0.3115	0.626	0.484	0.2704	0.3023	0.5980	0.4240	0.2480	0.2769
T-LLR	0.5660	0.4020	0.2322	0.2543	0.5280	0.3840	0.2223	0.2474	0.5160	0.3610	0.2162	0.2398
T-stemming	0.6040	0.4410	0.2507	0.2788	0.5640	0.4280	0.2388	0.2705	0.5660	0.4020	0.2320	0.2597
T-stemming-LLR	0.5280	0.3860	0.2206	0.2491	0.4980	0.3600	0.2087	0.2336	0.5160	0.3570	0.2121	0.2378
T+D	0.6660	0.4970	0.2809	0.3109	0.6500	0.4790	0.2716	0.2995	0.5880	0.4360	0.2460	0.2818
T+D+A+C	0.7300	0.5190	0.3090	0.3357	0.6860	0.5280	0.2995	0.3347	0.6460	0.4600	0.2678	0.2966
A+C	0.4800	0.2960	0.1534	0.1826	0.4500	0.2920	0.1463	0.1768	0.3400	0.2200	0.1148	0.1439
T+D+A+C-LLR	0.6360	0.4250	0.2402	0.2641	0.5740	0.3950	0.2213	0.2496	0.5400	0.3720	0.2105	0.2360
T+D+A+C-Pseudo	0.7300	0.5270	0.3170	0.3399	0.6520	0.4710	0.2731	0.3041	0.4920	0.3000	0.1836	0.1995
T-Pseudo	0.6420	0.4600	0.2690	0.2992	-	-	-	-	-	-	-	-

Table 8.2: Four measures (P5, P@10, MAP, Rpr) of title (T), title and description (T+D), all the fields (T+D+A+C) and attribute and categories (A+C) using log likelihood ratio for discriminative terms (LLR), stemming and pseudo relevance feedback(Pseudo) query models and all three retrieval strategies (BM25, TfIdf, LM) with click logs evaluation.

System	BM25				TfIdf				LM			
	P5	P10	MAP	Rpr	P5	P10	MAP	Rpr	P5	P10	MAP	Rpr
T	0.1680	0.1020	0.5653	0.5563	0.1540	0.0920	0.5305	0.5135	0.1660	0.0930	0.5610	0.5558
T-LLR	0.1580	0.0850	0.5341	0.5166	0.1500	0.0790	0.5125	0.4909	0.1540	0.0840	0.5314	0.5065
T-stemming	0.1640	0.0940	0.5584	0.5492	0.1600	0.0900	0.5376	0.5273	0.1660	0.0920	0.5582	0.5489
T-stemming-LLR	0.1580	0.0860	0.5374	0.5162	0.1460	0.0790	0.4868	0.4604	0.1560	0.0840	0.5295	0.5050
T+D	0.1700	0.1040	0.5619	0.5536	0.1600	0.0910	0.5321	0.5155	0.1680	0.0980	0.5629	0.5587
T+D+A+C	0.1720	0.0990	0.5764	0.5675	0.1580	0.0950	0.5644	0.5606	0.1700	0.0960	0.5726	0.5692
A+C	0.0920	0.0590	0.2987	0.2734	0.0600	0.0410	0.1810	0.1507	0.0900	0.0540	0.2946	0.2687
T+D+A+C-LLR	0.1600	0.0920	0.5389	0.5170	0.1540	0.0890	0.5220	0.5061	0.1640	0.0880	0.5351	0.5053
T+D+A+C-Pseudo	0.1720	0.0990	0.5741	0.5689	0.1500	0.0900	0.5298	0.5237	0.1620	0.0860	0.5496	0.5459
T-Pseudo	0.1180	0.0750	0.3787	0.3454	-	-	-	-	-	-	-	-

8.2 Late data fusion

Table 8.3: Four measures (P5, P@10, MAP, Rpr) of title (T), title and description (T+D), all the fields (T+D+A+C) and attribute and categories (A+C) using log likelihood ratio for discriminative terms (LLR), stemming and pseudo relevance feedback(Pseudo) query models and all three retrieval strategies (BM25, TfIdf, LM) and two types of ground truth (editorial and click logs).

System	Editorial				Click logs			
	P5	P10	MAP	Rpr	P5	P10	MAP	Rpr
combMAX	0.5400	0.3730	0.3426	0.2919	0.1280	0.0730	0.4393	0.4093
combMIN	0.0760	0.0460	0.0723	0.0359	0.0020	0.0020	0.0080	0.0012
combSUM	0.6160	0.4980	0.4589	0.4160	0.1720	0.1030	0.5683	0.5515
combMNZ	0.6460	0.5030	0.4688	0.4309	0.1720	0.1040	0.5619	0.5455
combANZ	0.0800	0.0490	0.0858	0.0374	0.0020	0.0020	0.0119	0.0018
WcombSUM	0.6140	0.4920	0.4511	0.4135	0.1740	0.1040	0.5636	0.5438
WcombMNZ	0.6360	0.5050	0.4663	0.4294	0.1740	0.1030	0.5621	0.5445
WcombWW	0.6320	0.5080	0.4657	0.4281	0.1740	0.1040	0.5630	0.5456

Table 8.4: Four measures (P5, P@10, MAP, Rpr) of combANZ with title (T), title and description (T+D), all the fields (T+D+A+C) and attribute and categories (A+C) using log likelihood ratio for discriminative terms (LLR), stemming and pseudo relevance feedback(Pseudo) query models and all three retrieval strategies (BM25, TfIdf, LM) and two types of ground truth (editorial and click logs).

System	Editorial				Click logs			
	P5	P10	MAP	Rpr	P5	P10	MAP	Rpr
T	0.2740	0.2600	0.2004	0.2561	0.0700	0.0570	0.1535	0.1010
T-LLR	0.2600	0.2440	0.1692	0.2289	0.0520	0.0520	0.1223	0.0764
T stemming	0.1520	0.1120	0.1242	0.1249	0.0180	0.0110	0.0662	0.0342
T-LLR stemming	0.0800	0.0620	0.0765	0.0680	0.0060	0.0070	0.0293	0.0036
T+D	0.2660	0.2090	0.1881	0.2160	0.0220	0.0210	0.0644	0.0164
T+D+A+C	0.2120	0.2190	0.1775	0.2368	0.0200	0.0320	0.0718	0.0161
A+C	0.1600	0.0990	0.0731	0.0849	0.0080	0.0090	0.0282	0.0091
T+D+A+C-LLR	0.1780	0.1670	0.1264	0.1754	0.0280	0.0340	0.0697	0.0160
T+D+A+C-Pseudo	0.1440	0.1400	0.1177	0.1122	0.0280	0.0300	0.0911	0.0549

8.3 Diversification

Table 8.5: Four measures (P5, P@10, MAP, Rpr) of title (T), title and description (T+D), all the fields (T+D+A+C) and attribute and categories (A+C) using log likelihood ratio for discriminative terms (LLR), stemming and pseudo relevance feedback(Pseudo) query models using MMR diversification method and three retrieval strategies (BM25, TfIdf, LM) with editorial evaluation.

System	BM25				TfIdf				LM			
	P5	P10	MAP	Rpr	P5	P10	MAP	Rpr	P5	P10	MAP	Rpr
T-	0.6580	0.4920	0.3404	0.3778	0.6080	0.4760	0.3267	0.3709	0.4520	0.3170	0.2425	0.2853
T-LLR	0.5600	0.3990	0.2717	0.3118	0.4880	0.3610	0.2457	0.2953	0.4300	0.3050	0.2134	0.2629
T-stemming	0.6100	0.4400	0.3080	0.3484	0.5500	0.4250	0.2884	0.3352	0.4240	0.2910	0.2224	0.2752
T-stemming-LLR	0.5240	0.3910	0.2621	0.3047	0.4620	0.3300	0.2365	0.2883	0.4340	0.2960	0.2091	0.2538
T+D	0.6700	0.4930	0.3421	0.3801	0.6080	0.4470	0.3159	0.3590	0.4540	0.3300	0.2413	0.2889
T+D+A+C	0.7300	0.5200	0.3596	0.3957	0.6660	0.5060	0.3501	0.3933	0.4960	0.3520	0.2605	0.3103
A+C	0.4460	0.2870	0.1625	0.2017	0.3440	0.2350	0.1427	0.1886	0.2460	0.1820	0.1009	0.1470
T+D+A+C-LLR	0.5820	0.4130	0.2699	0.3087	0.4940	0.3640	0.2418	0.2911	0.4540	0.3160	0.2160	0.2697
T+D+A+C-Pseudo	0.7400	0.5340	0.3835	0.4160	0.6460	0.4710	0.3285	0.3700	0.2380	0.1820	0.1284	0.1849
T-Pseudo	0.6800	0.4840	0.3239	0.3604	-	-	-	-	-	-	-	-

Table 8.6: Four measures (P5, P@10, MAP, Rpr) of title (T), title and description (T+D), all the fields (T+D+A+C) and attribute and categories (A+C) using log likelihood ratio for discriminative terms (LLR), stemming and pseudo relevance feedback(Pseudo) query models using MMR diversification method and three retrieval strategies (BM25, TfIdf, LM) with click logs evaluation.

System	BM25				TfIdf				LM			
	P5	P10	MAP	Rpr	P5	P10	MAP	Rpr	P5	P10	MAP	Rpr
T	0.1680	0.1020	0.5650	0.5563	0.1580	0.0930	0.5341	0.5213	0.1540	0.0860	0.5251	0.4981
T-LLR	0.1580	0.0840	0.5377	0.5277	0.1460	0.0800	0.5101	0.5014	0.1440	0.0790	0.5001	0.4785
T-stemming	0.1660	0.0940	0.5587	0.5487	0.1580	0.0890	0.5362	0.5268	0.1460	0.0800	0.5210	0.5019
T-stemming-LLR	0.1620	0.0860	0.5397	0.5329	0.1380	0.0780	0.4657	0.4382	0.1460	0.0810	0.5103	0.4998
T+D	0.1700	0.1060	0.5633	0.5547	0.1580	0.0890	0.5324	0.5189	0.1440	0.0820	0.5309	0.5165
T+D+A+C	0.1760	0.1000	0.5772	0.5697	0.1580	0.0950	0.5555	0.5451	0.1560	0.0900	0.5539	0.5411
A+C	0.0900	0.0580	0.2957	0.2634	0.0480	0.0360	0.1448	0.1102	0.0640	0.0410	0.2181	0.1835
T+D+A+C-LLR	0.1560	0.0920	0.5410	0.5270	0.1420	0.0840	0.4911	0.4693	0.1480	0.0850	0.5108	0.4904
T+D+A+C Pseudo	0.1720	0.0990	0.5742	0.5689	0.1500	0.0890	0.5239	0.5121	0.1060	0.0680	0.3990	0.3501
T-Pseudo	0.1180	0.0740	0.3780	0.3448	-	-	-	-	-	-	-	-

Table 8.7: Four measures (P5, P@10, MAP, Rpr) of title (T), title and description (T+D), all the fields (T+D+A+C) and attribute and categories (A+C) using log likelihood ratio for discriminative terms (LLR), stemming and pseudo relevance feedback(Pseudo) query models using MMRalt1 diversification method and three retrieval strategies (BM25, TfIdf, LM) with editorial evaluation.

System	BM25				TfIdf				LM			
	P5	P10	MAP	Rpr	P5	P10	MAP	Rpr	P5	P10	MAP	Rpr
T	0.6540	0.4890	0.3458	0.3846	0.5120	0.4150	0.2593	0.3162	0.4160	0.3120	0.2036	0.2491
T-LLR	0.5680	0.3980	0.2766	0.3175	0.4460	0.3350	0.2050	0.2599	0.3600	0.2700	0.1710	0.2226
T-stemming	0.6020	0.4400	0.3155	0.3518	0.4080	0.2970	0.1778	0.2192	0.3740	0.2790	0.1813	0.2341
T-stemming-LLR	0.5260	0.3870	0.2681	0.3121	0.2160	0.1600	0.0929	0.1257	0.3520	0.2630	0.1616	0.2068
T+D	0.6660	0.4950	0.3488	0.3844	0.5780	0.4440	0.2893	0.3384	0.4420	0.3320	0.2080	0.2594
T+D+A+C	0.7320	0.5180	0.3658	0.3994	0.5800	0.4430	0.2883	0.3363	0.4580	0.3640	0.2254	0.2855
A+C	0.4600	0.2930	0.1688	0.2088	0.3480	0.2350	0.1283	0.1652	0.2080	0.1540	0.0738	0.1127
T+D+A+C-LLR	0.6180	0.4200	0.2770	0.3138	0.4280	0.3150	0.1938	0.2455	0.3720	0.2700	0.1597	0.2113
T+D+A+C-Pseudo	0.7320	0.5240	0.3847	0.4153	0.5420	0.4090	0.2681	0.3100	0.2660	0.1970	0.1135	0.1503
T-Pseudo	0.6400	0.4600	0.3128	0.3534	-	-	-	-	-	-	-	-

Table 8.8: Four measures (P5, P@10, MAP, Rpr) of title (T), title and description (T+D), all the fields (T+D+A+C) and attribute and categories (A+C) using log likelihood ratio for discriminative terms (LLR), stemming and pseudo relevance feedback(Pseudo) query models using MMRalt1 diversification method and three retrieval strategies (BM25, TfIdf, LM) with click logs evaluation.

System	BM25				TfIdf				LM			
	P5	P10	MAP	Rpr	P5	P10	MAP	Rpr	P5	P10	MAP	Rpr
T	0.1680	0.1010	0.5653	0.5563	0.0480	0.0360	0.0704	0.0388	0.0440	0.0280	0.0561	0.0319
T-LLR	0.1580	0.0850	0.5351	0.5166	0.0480	0.0310	0.0899	0.0621	0.0380	0.0280	0.0786	0.0563
T-stemming	0.1660	0.0950	0.5588	0.5492	0.0400	0.0250	0.0649	0.0349	0.0420	0.0280	0.0632	0.0418
T-stemming-LLR	0.1580	0.0850	0.5383	0.5178	0.0240	0.0180	0.0502	0.0399	0.0400	0.0310	0.0927	0.0726
T+D	0.1720	0.1050	0.5627	0.5553	0.0420	0.0330	0.0531	0.0372	0.0560	0.0340	0.0581	0.0341
T+D+A+C	0.1720	0.0990	0.5765	0.5687	0.0420	0.0340	0.0540	0.0372	0.0380	0.0360	0.0513	0.0354
A+C	0.0900	0.0590	0.3002	0.2734	0.0220	0.0250	0.0565	0.0183	0.0280	0.0220	0.0626	0.0344
T+D+A+C-LLR	0.1600	0.0920	0.5376	0.5165	0.0380	0.0310	0.0699	0.0437	0.0500	0.0330	0.0812	0.0552
T+D+A+C-Pseudo	0.1720	0.0990	0.5741	0.5689	0.0360	0.0350	0.0521	0.0341	0.0340	0.0220	0.0405	0.0280
T-Pseudo	0.1180	0.0750	0.3788	0.3454	-	-	-	-	-	-	-	-

Table 8.9: Four measures (P5, P@10, MAP, Rpr) of title (T), title and description (T+D), all the fields (T+D+A+C) and attribute and categories (A+C) using log likelihood ratio for discriminative terms (LLR), stemming and pseudo relevance feedback(Pseudo) query models using MMRalt2 diversification method and three retrieval strategies (BM25, TfIdf, LM) with editorial evaluation.

System	BM25				TfIdf				LM			
	P5	P10	MAP	Rpr	P5	P10	MAP	Rpr	P5	P10	MAP	Rpr
T	0.6560	0.4860	0.3424	0.3798	0.5020	0.4000	0.2571	0.3175	0.3420	0.2700	0.1783	0.2332
T-LLR	0.5500	0.3790	0.2693	0.3096	0.4140	0.3110	0.1895	0.2502	0.2940	0.2130	0.1448	0.1960
T-stemming	0.6040	0.4330	0.3130	0.3533	0.4120	0.3060	0.1796	0.2269	0.2760	0.2180	0.1512	0.2078
T-stemming-LLR	0.5200	0.3730	0.2624	0.3033	0.1980	0.1430	0.0822	0.1180	0.2620	0.2020	0.1376	0.1840
T+D	0.6580	0.4820	0.3426	0.3836	0.5580	0.4140	0.2785	0.3217	0.3360	0.2520	0.1757	0.2254
T+D+A+C	0.7240	0.5170	0.3640	0.3971	0.5580	0.4140	0.2785	0.3217	0.3840	0.2940	0.1943	0.2535
A+C	0.4480	0.2920	0.1674	0.2084	0.3060	0.2110	0.1132	0.1599	0.2300	0.1560	0.0775	0.1153
T+D+A+C-LLR	0.6080	0.4130	0.2746	0.3102	0.4020	0.3020	0.1858	0.2390	0.3380	0.2520	0.1486	0.2147
T+D+A+C-Pseudo	0.7180	0.5200	0.3765	0.4086	0.5300	0.3880	0.2586	0.2980	0.1780	0.1430	0.0827	0.1364
T-Pseudo	0.6440	0.4640	0.3135	0.3531	-	-	-	-	-	-	-	-

Table 8.10: Four measures (P5, P@10, MAP, Rpr) of title (T), title and description (T+D), all the fields (T+D+A+C) and attribute and categories (A+C) using log likelihood ratio for discriminative terms (LLR), stemming and pseudo relevance feedback(Pseudo) query models using MMRalt2 diversification method and three retrieval strategies (BM25, TfIdf, LM) with click logs evaluation.

System	BM25				TfIdf				LM			
	P5	P10	MAP	Rpr	P5	P10	MAP	Rpr	P5	P10	MAP	Rpr
T	0.1680	0.0990	0.5647	0.5557	0.0580	0.0420	0.1063	0.0837	0.0280	0.0250	0.0573	0.0343
T-LLR	0.1540	0.0850	0.5343	0.5176	0.0380	0.0290	0.0835	0.0631	0.0340	0.0220	0.0782	0.0540
T-stemming	0.1660	0.0950	0.5582	0.5481	0.0640	0.0370	0.1513	0.1222	0.0280	0.0180	0.0614	0.0284
T-stemming-LLR	0.1600	0.0850	0.5361	0.5218	0.0200	0.0160	0.0532	0.0406	0.0360	0.0230	0.0927	0.0654
T+D	0.1700	0.1010	0.5605	0.5519	0.0400	0.0340	0.0510	0.0355	0.0320	0.0190	0.0607	0.0298
T+D+A+C	0.1720	0.0990	0.5773	0.5693	0.0400	0.0340	0.0510	0.0355	0.0440	0.0270	0.0641	0.0390
A+C	0.0920	0.0590	0.2977	0.2734	0.0280	0.0270	0.0576	0.0217	0.0280	0.0220	0.0695	0.0200
T+D+A+C-LLR	0.1620	0.0900	0.5385	0.5166	0.0400	0.0280	0.0800	0.0616	0.0420	0.0330	0.0936	0.0636
T+D+A+C-Pseudo	0.1560	0.0930	0.4806	0.4506	0.0360	0.0320	0.0503	0.0324	0.0160	0.0130	0.0416	0.0180
T-Pseudo	0.1200	0.0740	0.3788	0.3454	-	-	-	-	-	-	-	-

Table 8.11: Four measures (P5, P@10, MAP, Rpr) of title (T), title and description (T+D), all the fields (T+D+A+C) and attribute and categories (A+C) using log likelihood ratio for discriminative terms (LLR), stemming and pseudo relevance feedback(Pseudo) query models using MMRaltAvgLast4 diversification method and three retrieval strategies (BM25, TfIdf, LM) with editorial evaluation.

System	BM25				TfIdf				LM			
	P5	P10	MAP	Rpr	P5	P10	MAP	Rpr	P5	P10	MAP	Rpr
T	0.6460	0.4900	0.3435	0.3825	0.5140	0.4060	0.2616	0.3198	0.3360	0.2490	0.1706	0.2233
T-LLR	0.5460	0.3820	0.2709	0.3140	0.4060	0.3230	0.1917	0.2535	0.2820	0.2130	0.1434	0.1911
T-stemming	0.6000	0.4420	0.3137	0.3505	0.3980	0.3030	0.1792	0.2260	0.2900	0.2290	0.1531	0.2086
T-stemming-LLR	0.5080	0.3730	0.2615	0.3066	0.2020	0.1440	0.0867	0.1251	0.2740	0.2110	0.1390	0.1928
T+D	0.6540	0.4810	0.3422	0.3809	0.5560	0.4260	0.2842	0.3338	0.3420	0.2530	0.1731	0.2231
T+D+A+C	0.7200	0.5200	0.3640	0.4028	0.5560	0.4260	0.2842	0.3338	0.3700	0.2980	0.1915	0.2494
A+C	0.4260	0.2930	0.1673	0.2089	0.2980	0.2050	0.1137	0.1517	0.1820	0.1380	0.0721	0.1092
T+D+A+C-LLR	0.5760	0.4060	0.2722	0.3108	0.4080	0.3030	0.1873	0.2377	0.3240	0.2360	0.1446	0.1989
T+D+A+C-Pseudo	0.7140	0.5220	0.3760	0.4098	0.5060	0.3860	0.2591	0.3052	0.1460	0.1300	0.0786	0.1285
T-Pseudo	0.6380	0.4650	0.3126	0.3530	-	-	-	-	-	-	-	-

Table 8.12: Four measures (P5, P@10, MAP, Rpr) of title (T), title and description (T+D), all the fields (T+D+A+C) and attribute and categories (A+C) using log likelihood ratio for discriminative terms (LLR), stemming and pseudo relevance feedback(Pseudo) query models using MMRaltAvgLast4 diversification method and three retrieval strategies (BM25, TfIdf, LM) with click logs evaluation.

	BM25				TfIdf				LM			
System	P5	P10	MAP	Rpr	P5	P10	MAP	Rpr	P5	P10	MAP	Rpr
T	0.1660	0.1000	0.5645	0.5547	0.0560	0.0410	0.0982	0.0743	0.0380	0.0240	0.0509	0.0347
T-LLR	0.1580	0.0860	0.5353	0.5166	0.0380	0.0300	0.0854	0.0621	0.0320	0.0200	0.0724	0.0517
T-stemming	0.1660	0.0930	0.5587	0.5481	0.0600	0.0370	0.1503	0.1232	0.0320	0.0200	0.0529	0.0311
T-stemming-LLR	0.1540	0.0850	0.5353	0.5201	0.0240	0.0140	0.0541	0.0433	0.0360	0.0240	0.0890	0.0634
T+D	0.1700	0.1020	0.5616	0.5519	0.0420	0.0330	0.0514	0.0377	0.0380	0.0220	0.0522	0.0323
T+D+A+C	0.1740	0.0990	0.5770	0.5692	0.0420	0.0330	0.0514	0.0377	0.0340	0.0280	0.0498	0.0308
A+C	0.0920	0.0590	0.2983	0.2734	0.0260	0.0200	0.0509	0.0190	0.0220	0.0210	0.0566	0.0215
T+D+A+C-LLR	0.1600	0.0910	0.5373	0.5147	0.0400	0.0290	0.0801	0.0614	0.0400	0.0290	0.0844	0.0602
T+D+A+C-Pseudo	0.1560	0.0930	0.4804	0.4506	0.0340	0.0320	0.0511	0.0347	0.0160	0.0120	0.0348	0.0164
T-Pseudo	0.1180	0.0740	0.3782	0.3454	-	-	-	-	-	-	-	-

8.4 Data fusion of diversified result lists

Table 8.13: Four measures (P@5, P@10, MAP, Rpr) of late data fusion methods (combMAX, combMIN, combSUM, combMNZ, combANZ, WcombSUM, WcomMNZ, WcombWW) of fused system and fused diversified system using MMR approach and editorial ground truth.

System	P5	P10	MAP	Rpr
combANZ	0.0940	0.0860	0.1078	0.0826
compMAX	0.7320	0.5290	0.4679	0.4237
combMIN	0.0800	0.0570	0.0662	0.0358
combMNZ	0.6700	0.5290	0.4670	0.4400
combSUM	0.6700	0.5270	0.4669	0.4400
WcombMNZ	0.6560	0.5320	0.4649	0.4389
WcombSUM	0.6620	0.5400	0.4675	0.4399
WcompWW	0.6560	0.5370	0.4658	0.4412

Table 8.14: Four measures (P@5, P@10, MAP, Rpr) of late data fusion methods (combMAX, combMIN, combSUM, combMNZ, combANZ, Wcomb-SUM, WcomMNZ, WcombWW) of fused system and fused diversified system using MMRalt1 approach and editorial ground truth.

System	P5	P10	MAP	Rpr
combANZ	0.1320	0.1050	0.1184	0.0978
compMAX	0.7280	0.5380	0.4748	0.4279
combMIN	0.0820	0.0540	0.0662	0.0341
combMNZ	0.6760	0.5280	0.4762	0.4390
combSUM	0.6760	0.5280	0.4762	0.4390
WcombMNZ	0.6720	0.5250	0.4782	0.4415
WcombSUM	0.6740	0.5270	0.4815	0.4460
WcompWW	0.6740	0.5280	0.4814	0.4465

Table 8.15: Four measures (P@5, P@10, MAP, Rpr) of late data fusion methods (combMAX, combMIN, combSUM, combMNZ, combANZ, Wcomb-SUM, WcomMNZ, WcombWW) of fused system and fused diversified system using MMRalt2 approach and editorial ground truth.

System	P5	P10	MAP	Rpr
combANZ	0.1800	0.1300	0.1417	0.1220
compMAX	0.7140	0.5390	0.4671	0.4256
combMIN	0.0800	0.0520	0.0660	0.0347
combMNZ	0.6700	0.5290	0.4753	0.4396
combSUM	0.6700	0.5290	0.4754	0.4396
WcombMNZ	0.6600	0.5240	0.4713	0.4411
WcombSUM	0.6640	0.5280	0.4739	0.4450
WcompWW	0.6680	0.5310	0.4794	0.4491

Table 8.16: Four measures (P@5, P@10, MAP, Rpr) of late data fusion methods (combMAX, combMIN, combSUM, combMNZ, combANZ, Wcomb-SUM, WcomMNZ, WcombWW) of fused system and fused diversified system using MMRAltAvgLast4 approach and editorial ground truth.

System	P5	P10	MAP	Rpr
combANZ	0.1760	0.1260	0.1374	0.1213
compMAX	0.7120	0.5410	0.4665	0.4280
combMIN	0.0800	0.0520	0.0656	0.0341
combMNZ	0.6720	0.5280	0.4753	0.4391
combSUM	0.6720	0.5280	0.4754	0.4391
WcombMNZ	0.6620	0.5230	0.4721	0.4420
WcombSUM	0.6620	0.5250	0.4749	0.4434
WcompWW	0.6640	0.5330	0.4811	0.4486

i want morebooks!

Buy your books fast and straightforward online - at one of the world's fastest growing online book stores! Environmentally sound due to Print-on-Demand technologies.

Buy your books online at
www.get-morebooks.com

Kaufen Sie Ihre Bücher schnell und unkompliziert online – auf einer der am schnellsten wachsenden Buchhandelsplattformen weltweit!
Dank Print-On-Demand umwelt- und ressourcenschonend produziert.

Bücher schneller online kaufen
www.morebooks.de

OmniScriptum Marketing DEU GmbH
Heinrich-Böcking-Str. 6-8
D - 66121 Saarbrücken
Telefax: +49 681 93 81 567-9

info@omniscriptum.de
www.omniscriptum.de

Printed by Books on Demand GmbH, Norderstedt / Germany